THE TIMEX SINCLAIR
2068
EXPLORED

Tim Hartnell

A Wiley Press Book
John Wiley & Sons, Inc.
New York • Chichester • Brisbane • Toronto • Singapore

Publisher: Judy V. Wilson
Editor: Theron Shreve
Composition & make-up: Cobb/Dunlop Publisher Services, Inc.

Library of Congress Cataloging in Publication Data

Hartnell, Tim.
       The Timex Sinclair 2068 explored.

       Includes index.
       1. Timex Sinclair 2068 (Computer)   I. Title.
II. Title: Timex Sinclair two thousand sixty eight explored.
QA76.8.T49H37 1984   001.64'2   83-1303
ISBN 0-471-89099-5

Printed in the United States of America

84 85 86   10 9 8 7 6 5 4 3 2 1

Contents

Foreword

A sheet of paper may carry the jottings of an idiot or a sonnet by Shakespeare, but by itself it is nothing. In the same way a computer, however powerful it may be, is only what the programmer makes it, and therefore the skill and art of programming has risen to great importance. Hence this book, which takes over where the manual provided with the Timex Sinclair 2068 leaves off. No manual can say it all, and ours can only give the basics of programming. This book, by means of program examples, teaches skills of programming which, without its aid, might take years to acquire. It will be of great benefit both to the reader who has recently taken up programming and to the more experienced programmer who wishes to increase his skills.

Clive Sinclair

Acknowledgments

A number of people helped me write this book, and I would like to thank them most sincerely for lending their expertise. This has enabled me to make the book far more comprehensive than it would have been if I had relied only on my own resources. Several books, which are mentioned at the end of the chapters they apply to, also proved useful. They are listed as a guide to further reading if you wish to explore the subject matter of the chapter in more depth. Those who contributed to specific sections of the book are Mike Salem, managing director of Hilderbay, one of the leading firms creating and servicing ZX business software, who helped with the introduction to the business chapter and the "jargon" section of the appendixes; Jeff Warren, an experienced teacher and head of the educational software company CALPAC Computer Software, who provided the core of the text in the education chapter and five of the programs; Tim Rogers, a student from Richmond, who shares his enthusiasm for computer games writing in the games chapter, and who wrote NIGHTFALL, JACK-MAN, METEORS and BREAKOUT; Jeremy Ruston, another student, who has three books to his credit (*Pascal for Human Beings, The BBC Micro Revealed*, and *The Book of Listings*, a BBC Publications book which he cowrote with me) and who contributed the chapter on three-dimensional graphics; Dr. Tim Langdell, an experienced programmer from West Dulwich, who writes regularly for the British magazines *Your Computer* and *ZX Computing* and is currently conducting an Open University research project into machine intelligence, and who wrote the sound and color chapters; James Walsh, a student from Loughton, who is currently writing two books (one on building a computer from scratch, and the other a detailed guide to using machine code on the Spectrum) and who answers readers' questions for the magazine *Personal Computer World* and reviews software for my magazine *ZX Computing*, who contributed the chapter on machine code; and Gil Held, author of numerous Wiley Quick Reference guides, for his assistance with the technical changes made for the Timex Sinclair 2068. Finally, I must thank Clive Sinclair, not only for inventing the Spectrum and its predecessors, without which I and hundreds of thousands of others could never have afforded to enter the computer world, but also for his encouragement and assistance.

Introduction

Production of the Oxford University Press dictionary took over 70 years, because the compilers wanted to include every word in the English language, and every meaning of every word. I felt, when surveying the ground this book could cover, that writing *The Timex Sinclair 2068 Explored* could also take 70 years, if every possibility of the computer was catered for. Therefore, I selected what seemed to me to be the most important elements of programming on the 2068, and the areas in which you would be most likely to want to apply your computer, and drew up a book outline based on those conclusions.

Many of my computer books include a statement along the lines of "This is a doing book, not a reading one," by which I mean the book is to be regarded as a tool to direct hands-on computer use, rather than one to be read as you might read a novel. The same admonition applies to this book. While you may well get some benefit from just reading through it, the real value of the book will only be realized when you read it with your 2068 turned on, and when you enter each of the routines and programs when you come to them in the text.

Do not feel that there is any pressure on you to read the whole book from start to finish in the order in which it is presented. There may be things you already know, or at this stage have no desire to know. By all means, bypass these chapters the first time you work through the book, and then perhaps you can come back to them later.

Whatever you do, don't regard *The Timex Sinclair 2068 Explored* as a textbook. Textbooks seem to me to be pervaded by a sour air which renders their contents joyless, and that is the last thing I would want this book to be. It is a guidebook; a signpost; an indicator towards areas of computer use where real adventures lie. Please regard it as such. If you do, the book should help you get a great deal of pleasure from your 2068.

In this book, we start by looking at the fundamentals of programming, then go on to ways of adding color and sound to your programs, using the relevant commands to get the 2068 to produce effects which are more interesting than you may have thought possible.

Using the 2068 for business, and then in education, is covered next—with each chapter supplied with a number of fully developed programs—and then we have a major chapter on games. This chapter includes programs for several ready-to-run games, and should give you a number of ideas to help you create your own games. The production of user-defined graphics is also discussed in the games chapter.

An even more spectacular use of the 2068's high-resolution graphics is outlined in the next chapter for the production of three-dimensional graphics.

Finally, we look at the use of machine code on the 2068, and suggest ways of further developing your programming skills. In the appendixes you'll find a brief history of computers, an explanation of some of the jargon associated with them and an outline of the 2068's specifications.

All in all, I hope we've managed to produce for you a comprehensive guide to your Timex Sinclair 2068 which will help you make the most of your computer in the coming months.

Good programming,
Tim Hartnell,
London

1

Programming in BASIC

BASIC is the world's most popular programming language—because it is the easiest one to learn. Computer languages are spoken of in "levels"; a high level language is one which is close to English, a low level one is closer to the weird patterns of ones and zeros a computer understands.

BASIC is a high level language. Even if you have no experience of programming at this point, you'll be pleased to learn you already know quite a bit of BASIC.

Words like PRINT, STOP, and AND mean just about the same thing in BASIC as they do in English. So does IF and THEN and OR. I hope you can see already that programming is simpler than perhaps you had thought it would be.

Essentially, when you write a program, you give the Timex Sinclair a series of instructions to follow. The Timex Sinclair, like all computers built to date, has quite extraordinary calculating and decision-making abilities, but absolutely no imagination. If you tell the computer to do something, it will do it. If you leave out part of the instructions it will attempt to carry out the rest without realizing that something has been left out.

Imagine you had a robot servant, and you wanted it to draw a bath. GO TO BATH might be the first instruction in its program. IF BATH IS EMPTY THEN TURN ON TAP. IF BATH IS FULL THEN TURN TAP OFF. The robot would happily trundle to the bathroom, dip its electronic hand into the bath and discover it was empty, and then turn the tap on. It would

1

stand there forever, waiting for the water level to reach a point where it would be detected, so the tap could be turned off. But because you forgot to include an instruction like CHECK IF PLUG IN PLUGHOLE and IF PLUG NOT IN PLUGHOLE THEN PUT PLUG IN PLUGHOLE, the robot would not think to do this.

This is exactly how your Timex Sinclair works, by following *explicit* instructions from you. And believe it or not, with a few reservations, your computer could more or less follow the instructions or program you gave the robot . . . because those instructions contain a number of words of the BASIC programming language.

Here is a simple program for the Timex Sinclair which I am sure you can understand, even without any training in programming languages.

```
LET A = 20
LET B = A + A
IF B = 40 THEN PRINT "B EQUALS 40"
```

This is straightforward English, yet it is also BASIC. The first line of the program (LET A = 20) is simple, as is the second one (LET B = A + A). The third line looks remarkably similar to one of the earlier robot instructions such as IF BATH IS EMPTY THEN TURN ON TAP; IF B = 40 THEN PRINT "B EQUALS 40". You could almost type this program into your Timex Sinclair, and it would work, with the Timex Sinclair printing up instantly B EQUALS 40.

The only thing these three lines need to turn them into a program is a number before each line. The following is a program which the Timex Sinclair would act on.

```
10 LET A = 20
20 LET B = A + A
30 IF B = 40 THEN PRINT "B EQUALS 40"
```

The line numbers can be any numbers you choose (between 1 and 9999). The computer automatically sorts them into order. We tend to number programs in steps of 10 because it leaves room between the lines if we decide to add something else in later.

So you see, already you've had some experience in the BASIC programming words LET, IF . . . THEN and PRINT. The equals sign and the plus sign you will know from ordinary arithmetic. In many cases, they behave in BASIC just like they do in ordinary sums.

Before we actually plug in the computer and do some programming, I'd like to introduce you to another word in BASIC which, as you'll discover in a moment, you already know. In fact the word is really two words—GO and TO.

In BASIC they always come together as GO TO, and are available from a single key on the Timex Sinclair (the G key). You'll recall we had our robot start the bath-drawing program by saying GO TO BATH. In the world of computer programming, we say GO TO a line number. We could add a final line, 40, to our three-line program above which reads:

```
40   GO TO 30
```

This would mean that the computer would execute line 30, and print out B EQUALS 40 then would move on, in sequence, to line 40, where it would find the instruction GO TO 30. Without questioning why you have told it to do this, the computer would follow instructions, and GO TO line 30, where it would find the instruction to print out B EQUALS 40 which it would do. It would then proceed to line 40 where once again it would strike the instruction GO TO 30 . . . and of course it would do so, until the end of time, or until the screen was full of lines, each line containing the statement B EQUALS 40.

We can proceed no further without having the Timex Sinclair turned on, so get out your computer and—following the instructions given in the manual—plug it into the power supply and the television set.

The keyboard on the Timex Sinclair looks forbidding when you first tackle it—all those funny words like MERGE and VERIFY, and the mathematical terms including SIN and COS which you had hoped you'd left behind forever at school. Don't worry. Once you know your way around the keyboard, you'll find it remarkably simple to control, and in the words of the advertisement for the Timex Sinclair's predecessor, "within days you'll be talking to it like an old friend."

THE KEYBOARD

Two of the most important parts of the keyboard are the shift keys. They are on the bottom row, the CAPS SHIFT (in white) in the bottom left hand corner, and SYMBOL SHIFT (in black) third from the right in the bottom right hand corner. These keys determine what you are going to get when you press the other keys, with their bewildering array of words and symbols.

I'll assume from now on that your computer is turned on. Press any of the white alphabet keys, and you'll see the word written on the key (such as LOAD, LIST or PRINT) appear. This is a "keyword." One of the ways the Timex Sinclair makes the best use of its memory, and a feature which makes it very easy to program, is the keyword system. Simply pressing a key produces the whole word from that key. On most other computers you have to type in a word like LIST, DIM or FOR in full. Hold down the CAPS SHIFT key, and press the DELETE key (top right hand corner) until everything you've typed in so far has been erased.

Now, press the P key, and the word PRINT will appear. Then, press any of the number keys, so you have something like PRINT 62735 at the bottom of the screen. Now press the key marked ENTER (right hand side, one up from the bottom). The screen will clear and the number you've requested will appear at the top of the screen. The computer has obeyed your instruction to PRINT a number. The Timex Sinclair generally waits until you have pressed ENTER before actually doing anything.

We'll enter a simple program, to show the keyword system in use. Type in the following, after holding down the CAPS SHIFT and pressing the 2 key (CAPS LOCK) to get capital letters in the program.

```
10 INPUT      (just press the I key) A
              (now press ENTER to show you've finished the prog-
              ram line)
20 PRINT A    (press ENTER)
30 GO TO 10   (press ENTER)
```

Note that the word PRINT comes from the P key, and GO TO from the G key. The spaces in the program listing are added automatically. Once you have this in your computer, we can make it work, by pressing the R key, which will make the word RUN appear, and then pressing ENTER. A flashing cursor will appear at the bottom of the screen, showing the computer is waiting for a number. Enter any number, then press ENTER. You'll see your number appear at the top of the screen. You know from the discussion of GO TO BATH we had earlier, that the final line of the program (line 30) sends action back to line 10, so the computer will continue to execute this program loop forever, or until we stop it. You can stop this program by entering any letter when the Timex Sinclair is waiting for a number. The computer will stop, printing an error message at the bottom of the screen.

Once you've stopped the program, touch the A key then press ENTER, and the screen will go black, and then clear, with the copyright notice at the bottom of the screen. The keyword available from the A key is NEW, which wipes everything in the computer's memory, so you must use it with care.

So, you've learned that the white keywords are obtained by pressing the key required after you have entered a line number. Let's look at the words in the black band *on* the keys. Hold down the SYMBOL SHIFT key, and then press the Y key. You'll see the word AND appear. Still holding down the SYMBOL SHIFT, press the G, and THEN will appear. So the words in the black bands *on* the keys, and the symbols like + and $, are obtained by holding down the SYMBOL SHIFT, then pressing the required key.

You get the words *above* the keys by pressing down both shift keys together, then letting them go, and touching the key required. Try it now. Press down the CAPS SHIFT and the SYMBOL SHIFT keys together, let them go, then touch the A key. The word READ should appear.

It is a little more difficult to get the words *under* the keys. Press down both shift keys together, then release the CAPS SHIFT, but do not let go of the SYMBOL SHIFT. Then press the X key. The word INK should appear. You may have to practice this a little to ensure you get the word INK (or BEEP, PAPER, FLASH or BRIGHT) every time.

Read through this whole section again, doing each of the exercises, until you're sure you understand it. Don't worry if it seems to take a long time at present. You'll be pleasantly surprised at how quickly you will learn the keyboard system. At the end of this introductory chapter we have a program designed to teach you where the alphabetical keys on the Timex Sinclair are, to encourage "touch typing," but first I want to introduce you to the first real program in this book. It may take you a while to type in, but please persevere. Once you've entered the whole of this program into your computer, press RUN and play the game against the computer.

The program plays ROCK, SCISSORS and PAPER, a computer version of the human game in which two players hide their hands behind their backs, and bring out a hand making a symbol for rock (a closed fist), scissors (two fingers pointing) or paper (open hand). Rock beats scissors (because a rock can blunt scissors), scissors beat paper (because scissors can cut paper) and paper beats rock (because paper can wrap a rock). You enter your choice of ROCK, SCISSORS or PAPER in this program by entering the numbers 1, 2 or 3. The choice they represent is shown at the top of the screen.

Before you enter the program, the following comments may help. The equals sign (first used in line 30) is from the L key. You get it by holding down SYMBOL SHIFT, then pressing L. Remember to press ENTER after each program line is written, to get it to move from the bottom of the screen into the program proper at the top. If the line refuses to move up, a flashing question mark will appear somewhere in the line. This is the computer's sign to you that you have made a mistake in the line. Look carefully at the point where the question mark is flashing to discover your mistake.

The colon (:) after the word CLS (which stands for Clear the Screen) in line 60 is found on the Z key. Hold down the SYMBOL SHIFT and press Z to get it. Line 70 has a single apostrophe (') after the word PRINT, before the opening quote marks ("). You'll find the single apostrophe on the 7 key, and it is obtained by holding down the SYMBOL SHIFT, and pressing the 7. The double quotes come from the P key.

You need to exercise a little care to get line 170 into your computer correctly. After 170 LET C=, you need the word INT which is not typed in letter by letter, but is obtained from the R key. Press both shift keys, release them, then press R and INT will appear. The open bracket is on the 8 key (hold down SYMBOL SHIFT while pressing the 8 key) and the word RND is available from the T key. Press both shift keys at once, release them, then press T. The asterisk (*), which stands for multiply in BASIC, comes from the B key, and is obtained by holding down SYMBOL SHIFT as you press B.

Do not try to spell out words like AND, OR, THEN and TO, but find them on the keys. These words are obtained by holding down SYMBOL SHIFT, then pressing the relevant key.

Now, enter the program, then return to the book.

ROCK, SCISSORS, PAPER

```
  10 REM ROCK, SCISSORS, PAPER
  20 REM © HARTNELL, 1982
  30 LET COMP=0
  40 LET HUM=0
  50 FOR A=1 TO 10
  60 CLS : PRINT "ROUND NUMBER "
;A
  70 PRINT '"1 - ROCK"
  80 PRINT "2 - SCISSORS"
  90 PRINT "3 - PAPER"
 100 PRINT '"ENTER 1, 2 OR 3"
 110 INPUT B
 120 PRINT '"YOU PICKED ";
 130 IF B=1 THEN PRINT "ROCK"
 140 IF B=2 THEN PRINT "SCISSORS
"
 150 IF B=3 THEN PRINT "PAPER"
 160 PAUSE 50
 170 LET C=INT (RND*3)+1
 180 PRINT '"I PICKED ";
 190 IF C=1 THEN PRINT "ROCK"
 200 IF C=2 THEN PRINT "SCISSORS
"
 210 IF C=3 THEN PRINT "PAPER"
 220 LET D=260
 230 IF B=C THEN PRINT '"IT'S A
DRAW!": GO TO D
 240 IF C=1 AND B=2 OR C=2 AND B
=3 OR C=3 AND B=1 THEN PRINT '"I
 WIN!": LET COMP=COMP+1: GO TO D
 250 IF B=1 AND C=2 OR B=2 AND C
=3 OR B=3 AND C=1 THEN PRINT '"Y
OU WIN!": LET HUM=HUM+1
 260 PRINT '"SCORE"''"ME> ";COMP
;TAB 10;"YOU> ";HUM
 270 PAUSE 100
 280 NEXT A
 290 IF HUM=COMP THEN PRINT '"T
HAT GAME WAS A DRAW!"
 300 IF HUM<COMP THEN PRINT '"I
WON THAT GAME!"
 310 IF COMP<HUM THEN PRINT '"Y
OU WON THAT GAME!"
```

This is part of a game in progress:

```
ROUND NUMBER 7

1 - ROCK
2 - SCISSORS
3 - PAPER

ENTER 1, 2 OR 3

YOU PICKED PAPER

I PICKED SCISSORS

I WIN!

SCORE

ME> 2      YOU> 3
```

I'll go through the program line by line, to try and explain what is happening in each line.

10   This line starts with REM, which stands for REMark. REM statements are included in programs only for the benefit of humans reading the program listing. The computer ignores everything that appears in a line after the word REM.

20   This is another REM statement, also ignored by the computer.

30   LET means much the same in BASIC as it does in English. The word COMP (short for computer) is called a *variable*, which is any combination of letters and numbers (starting with a *letter*) which is *assigned* (or made equal to) a numerical value. COMP holds the computer's score, and it is set equal to zero at the start of the game.

40   This line does the same for a variable called HUM, for the human's score.

50   FOR . . . This is the start of what is called a "FOR/NEXT loop." The computer generally goes through such a loop the number of times indicated by the last number in the FOR statement. Look down to line 280 (NEXT A). This is the end of the FOR/NEXT loop. In this program, the computer runs the gauntlet from line 50 to line 280 ten times, carrying out all the instructions within the program as it does so.

60   CLS, as mentioned before, Clears the Screen. The colon (:) allows you to add a second statement to the line. PRINT does just that, printing the words in quote marks following the command PRINT. As well as that, the computer prints the *value* of A. The first time through the FOR/NEXT loop A is equal to 1, the second time to 2, and so on until A equals 10 the last time through the loop. So PRINT "ROUND NUMBER", A produces ROUND NUMBER 4, or whatever number A is equal to, on the screen.

70–90   These three lines print the numbers 1 to 3, and the word (such as ROCK) they represent. Note the apostrophe (from the 7 key) before the opening quotes in line 70. This moves the print position down a line, so that there is a blank line on the screen between the words ROUND NUMBER 4 and 1— ROCK.

100   The apostrophe is used again to put a blank line before ENTER 1, 2 OR 3 is printed.

110   The INPUT command waits until a number is entered by the user. In this case, the number you enter is assigned to the variable B.

120   This prints YOU PICKED.

130–150   These three lines interpret the number you've entered (1, 2 or 3—assigned to B) and decide which word (ROCK, SCIS-

SORS or PAPER) this stands for, and prints it up on the screen.

160   PAUSE. This puts a short delay into the program, to make it look as if the computer is "thinking." The number after the word PAUSE is in sixtieths of a second, so PAUSE 50 is a delay of five-sixths of a second. PAUSE 0 will wait forever, or until any key is pressed.

170   This is a very interesting line, in which the computer generates a random number. Random numbers are very useful in games programs. The RND function (both shift keys, then press T) generates a random number between 0 and 1. You can show this by typing in PRINT RND, then pressing ENTER. You'll get a number between 1 and 0. Line 170 turns it into a whole number in the range one to three. If the 3 which follows the asterisk within the brackets was changed to, say, a 10, then C would be set equal to a number chosen at random by the computer between 1 and 10. However, in this case we want the computer to choose 1, 2 or 3, so we multiply RND by three.

180   This begins the statement to tell you what the computer has chosen.

190–210 These lines change the 1, 2 or 3 which C has been set equal to into ROCK, SCISSORS or PAPER.

220   The variable D is set equal to 260. This is so, at the end of lines 230 and 240 (GO TO D), the computer will GO TO line 260. The Timex Sinclair is quite happy to GO TO results of calculations, so you could (although it would serve no purpose) end lines 230 and 240 with GO TO 2*130 (two times 130).

230   If B and C are the same number, the computer knows that it and you have chosen the same thing, so prints IT'S A DRAW, then GOes TO D (i.e. GOes TO 260).

240   This complicated looking line determines if the combinations of C and B result in a win for the computer. IF they do THEN the computer PRINTs I WIN and adds one to its score (LET COMP = COMP + 1). Although this statement looks a little odd when compared with normal arithmetic, it really means "make the variable named on the left hand side of the equals sign equal in value to the old value of the variable, plus one." Don't worry if you don't understand this right now because the reason for it will gradually become clear as you use lines like this more often.

250   This checks the human win condition, and if it finds it, adds one to the human score (LET HUM = HUM +1).

260   This prints out the score. Notice that there is a single apostrophe before the opening quote marks, and two single apostrophes after the quotes which follow SCORE and before the quotes which precede ME. As you've no doubt seen from running the program, this puts *two* blank lines in before the line starting ME is printed. The pointing arrow head, the "greater than" symbol, which follows the words ME and YOU is obtained from the T key, when you press it while holding down the SYMBOL SHIFT key.

270   This PAUSEs for just under two seconds so you can read the result of the round.

280   NEXT A is the end of the FOR/NEXT loop which started in line 50. As explained earlier, this sends action all the way back to line 50, where the value of A is increased by one, and then the following lines are executed in order.

290   If the value assigned to the variable HUM is the same as the value assigned to the variable COMP, then the Timex Sinclair knows that the game is a draw, and prints up the message (after skipping two lines, using two single apostrophes) "THAT GAME WAS A DRAW".

300   IF HUM is less than COMP, then the computer knows that it has won.

310   IF COMP is less than HUM, then the computer knows that you have won.

I hope this explanation does not seem too bewildering. I am trying to get across the fundamentals of programming the Timex Sinclair in BASIC in the simplest possible way, and a lot of ground must be covered in a short time.

ADDING A LITTLE COLOR

We'll be looking at ways of making the most of the Timex Sinclair's color capabilities (and sound) a little later in this book, but for now I'd like to introduce you to a few of the simplest uses of the color commands, so you can see how well these can be used to enhance programs. A new version of the ROCK, SCISSORS, PAPER program, with color commands added, follows. You can easily modify the program you now have by using the Timex Sinclair's edit facilities.

ROCK, SCISSORS, PAPER (WITH COLOR)

```
 10 REM ROCK, SCISSORS, PAPER
 20 REM © HARTNELL, 1982
 30 LET COMP=0
 40 LET HUM=0
 50 FOR A=1 TO 10
 60 CLS : PRINT INK 2;"ROUND NU
MBER "; INK 1;A
 70 PRINT INK 1;'"1 - ROCK"
 80 PRINT INK 2;"2 - SCISSORS"
 90 PRINT INK 3;"3 - PAPER"
100 PRINT INK 6; PAPER 2;'"ENTE
R 1, 2 OR 3"
```

```
110 INPUT B
120 PRINT INK B; '"YOU PICKED ";
130 IF B=1 THEN PRINT "ROCK"
140 IF B=2 THEN PRINT "SCISSORS
"
150 IF B=3 THEN PRINT "PAPER"
160 PAUSE 50
170 LET C=INT (RND*3)+1
180 PRINT INK C; '"I PICKED ";
190 IF C=1 THEN PRINT "ROCK"
200 IF C=2 THEN PRINT "SCISSORS
"
210 IF C=3 THEN PRINT "PAPER"
220 LET D=260
230 IF B=C THEN PRINT FLASH 1; '
"IT'S A DRAW!": GO TO D
240 IF C=1 AND B=2 OR C=2 AND B
=3 OR C=3 AND B=1 THEN PRINT FLA
SH 1; '"I WIN!": LET CO
MP=COMP+1: GO TO D
250 IF B=1 AND C=2 OR B=2 AND C
=3 OR B=3 AND C=1 THEN PRINT FLA
SH 1; '"YOU WIN!": LET HUM=HUM+1
260 PRINT '"SCORE"''"ME> ";COMP
;TAB 10;"YOU> ";HUM
270 PAUSE 100
280 NEXT A
285 INVERSE 1
290 IF HUM=COMP THEN PRINT '''"T
HAT GAME WAS A DRAW!"
300 IF HUM<COMP THEN PRINT '''"I
WON THAT GAME!"
310 IF COMP<HUM THEN PRINT '''"Y
OU WON THAT GAME!"
```

You'll see in line 60 the words INK 2 have been added. To get these into the line, press LIST (the K key) then 60, so you have LIST 60, then press ENTER. The word 'scroll?' will appear at the bottom of the screen. Press N to stop the listing scrolling further, then hold down the CAPS SHIFT key, and press the 1 key, which has the word EDIT above it. The line the cursor (a greater than sign) is pointing to (in this case, line 60) will appear at the bottom of the screen. We want to insert the words INK 2 after the word PRINT, so holding down the CAPS SHIFT, press the 8 key. You'll see the cursor move across in the direction of the arrow on the 8 key. Once the cursor has gone past PRINT, but before it goes any further, take your finger off the 8 key. Now, press down both shift keys at once, and then release the CAPS SHIFT key. Still holding the SYMBOL SHIFT key down, press the X key, and—if all is well—the word INK should appear. Follow this with a 2, then a semicolon (SYMBOL SHIFT, then the O key), and then press ENTER again. You'll see the amended line take the place of the original line 60.

RUN the program again, and you'll see the words ROUND NUMBER 1 appear in red. The colors are chosen by the numbers zero to seven (as will be explained in more detail later). INK 1 will cause the letters following it to be blue, 2 will turn them red, and so on. (You don't need to run a whole game through before continuing. Just enter a Q when asked for your number, and the program will stop with a puzzled error message, because it doesn't know what Q means.)

Press EDIT (CAPS SHIFT and 1) again, and line 60 will reappear at the bottom of the screen. Using the CAPS SHIFT/8 combination, move the cursor across to go past the quotes after NUMBER and add INK 1, then another semicolon (which must join these extra commands in a PRINT statement together) before the A. Return the line to position within the program with ENTER and RUN the program again. You should see the words ROUND NUMBER appear in red, and the number 1 come up in blue.

If the colors are unclear, fiddle with the channel tuning, and the color control on your television, until you can see the red and blue properly. Different makes of television reproduce the colors differently, so you may find one color is more intense than the others.

You can now go through the whole program, making the necessary changes, to add color throughout. The lines which need to be modified are 60, 70, 80, 90, 100, 120, 180, 230, 240, 250 and 285 (which must be added—it will sort itself automatically into order). RUN the program again, and see how well the color commands enhance the program and give it life.

TOUCH-TYPING TUTOR

Our final program in this introductory chapter to the book is designed to help you find your way around the keyboard. When you RUN the program, it will put a number or a letter of the alphabet, chosen at random, on the screen in the approximate position it is on the keyboard. You have a limited time in which to press the designated key. If you get it wrong, the forgiving computer gives you another chance. You'll be pleased to see how quickly you'll learn the layout of the keyboard using this routine.

If you find you do not have enough time to find the keys when you first run this program, change the 100 in line 180 into a bigger number. Start with 300, and gradually decrease it until you feel the time is about right for your present level of typing prowess. Be careful to get the numbers and letters in the DATA statements (lines 80 to 110) correct, as these control where the various numbers and letters will be printed. After you've run through the program a few times, come back to this book for a line by line breakdown of it.

KEYBOARD TUTOR

```
10 REM          KEYBOARD TUTOR
20 DIM A$(36,5)
30 LET SCORE=0
40 FOR A=1 TO 36
50 READ B$
60 LET A$(A)=B$
70 NEXT A
```

```
  80 DATA "10502","20505","30508
","40611","50614","60617","70520
","80628","90526","00629"
  90 DATA "A1202","B1517","C1511
","D1208","E0908","F1211","G1214
","H1217","I0923","J1220"
 100 DATA "K1223","L1226","M1523
","N1520","O0926","P0929","Q0902
","R0911","S1205","T0914"
 110 DATA "U0920","V1514","W0905
","X1508","Y0917","Z1505"
 120 REM
 130 REM           THE TEST
 140 REM
 150 FOR A=1 TO 10: BEEP .02,-10
: CLS
 155 IF INKEY$<>"" THEN GO TO 15
5
 160 LET B=INT (RND*36)+1
 170 PRINT FLASH 1; PAPER 6;AT V
AL (A$(B)(2 TO 3)),VAL (A$(B)(4
TO )};A$(B,1)
 180 FOR C=1 TO 100
 190 LET C$=INKEY$
 200 IF C$<>"" THEN GO TO 260
 210 NEXT C
 220 PRINT AT 0,0; INK 7; PAPER
4; FLASH 1; BRIGHT 1;"YOU TOOK T
OO LONG"
 225 FOR D=1 TO 70: NEXT D
 230 NEXT A
 240 GO TO 300
 260 IF C$=A$(B,1) THEN LET SCOR
E=SCORE+1: BEEP .25,SCORE*4: PRI
NT AT 16,0; PAPER 6; INK 2;"WELL
 DONE. YOUR SCORE IS NOW ";SCORE
 265 IF C$<>A$(B,1) THEN PRINT A
T 0,0; INK 1; PAPER 6; FLASH 1;"
   SORRY, BUT THAT WAS WRONG";TA
B 10;"TRY AGAIN": GO TO 170
 270 FOR D=1 TO 100
 280 NEXT D
 290 NEXT A
 300 CLS : PRINT AT 8,2; FLASH 1
; BRIGHT 1; PAPER 6; INK 2;"YOUR
 SCORE WAS ";SCORE;" OUT OF 10"
 310 IF SCORE>7 THEN PRINT AT 10
,7; FLASH 1; INK 4; PAPER 7; BRI
GHT 1;"CONGRATULATIONS!"
```

10   This is a REM (remember REM stands for remark) statement which the computer ignores. Note you can put as many spaces in a REM statement as you like.

20   Line 20 sets up an array. An array is used when you want to store a list of numbers or words and refer to the item in the list by referring just to the position it occupies in the list. Line 20 sets up an array called A$. The dollar sign means that the items stored in the list are words, within quote marks, rather than numbers. The first *element* of the array is referred to as A$ (1), the second as A$ (2) and so on.

30   Sets a variable called SCORE to hold your score of the number of letters you find correctly.

40–70   This is a FOR/NEXT loop, as in the previous program. Line 50 (READ B$) acts in conjunction with the DATA statements (lines 80 to 110). It reads each of these in turn, one for each cycle through the loop. The first time through the loop it reads the first item in the DATA line ("10602") and *assigns* this to B$. Line 60 then assigns A$ (1) to this value of B$. The next time through the loop, when A equals two, so line 60 reads, in effect, LET A$(2)=B$, and this time B$ has the value of the second item in the DATA statement, "20605". This continues until all 36 items in the A$ list have been assigned a DATA statement.

80–110   The DATA statements. Notice that items are enclosed within quote marks, and separated by commas.

120–140   Three REM statements.

150   This sets up another FOR/NEXT loop. FOR/NEXT loops do not have to be called A; any letter of the alphabet is acceptable, so FOR J=1 TO 10 or FOR M=1 TO 10 would do as well. BEEP .02, − 10 makes a short sound (BEEP is discussed in detail later in the book), and CLS clears the screen.

155   INKEY$, which you'll find above the N key, reads the keyboard, waiting for a key to be pressed. This line waits until your hands are clear of the keyboard before continuing.

160   This sets B equal to a random number between 1 and 36, to choose one of the numbers 0 to 9, or a letter of the alphabet.

170   This is a fairly complex line, which prints the letter or number on the key A$(B,1), at its correct location, which is done by PRINTing AT the second and third numbers in the DATA statement down (so if the second and third numbers are 12, it would print 12 lines from the top), and the fourth and fifth numbers across (so if the fourth and fifth numbers in the DATA statement were 05, it would print 5 spaces across). In other words, each of the DATA statements contains either a letter or number as the first element, and the final four elements are its location on the screen, items two and three being the position down the screen, four and five the position across.

180–210   This FOR/NEXT loop waits a designated time for a keypress, the length of the delay being set by the number at the end of line 180. If a key has been pressed, line 200 detects this, and sends action to line 260.

220   If you don't press a key in time, the computer prints up the message YOU TOOK TOO LONG.

225   This is a short delay, using a FOR/NEXT loop. You can use PAUSE or an "empty" FOR/NEXT loop for a delay.

230   Sends action back to line 150 for the next test.

240   At the end of ten tries, sends the computer to line 300 to print out the final score.

260   Checks to see if the key pressed is the same as the one printed on the screen, and if it is adds one to the SCORE, and prints out the message WELL DONE, YOUR SCORE IS NOW 3, or whatever your score happens to be.

265   If the key pressed was not the same as the one shown on the screen, prints SORRY, BUT THAT WAS WRONG, TRY AGAIN, then sends action back to line 170 to let you try again. Notice that there is a single comma *after* the close quote marks following the words TRY AGAIN. Leave this comma out, and see how this changes the display.

270–280   This is a delay before the next letter or number is printed on the screen.

290   Sends action back to line 150.

300   Prints out the score.

310   Adds a congratulations message if a score greater than 7 has been achieved.

   You'll find this a very useful program to help you gain familiarity with the keyboard layout.

   The material in this chapter has been somewhat condensed but I hope that careful reading of it, and entering the programs at the right time, has given you a fair introduction to programming in BASIC on Timex Sinclair. This information should complement that given in the manual which came with your computer to help you become a proficient programmer fairly rapidly. The rest of the book will assume you have mastered the information given in this chapter, and that you understand the introductory manual and much of the early material in the second manual which came with your computer.

2

Exploring the Timex Sinclair's Color

The Timex Sinclair has six colors (dark blue, red, magenta, green, cyan, and yellow) plus black and white. Each color is given a number between 0 and 7. The relationship between colors and numbers is:

    0   Black
    1   Dark blue
    2   Red
    3   Magenta (a sort of pinkish purple)
    4   Green
    5   Cyan (a light blue)
    6   Yellow
    7   White

If you have a black and white television, or turn the color control right down on your color TV, you'll see these colors, printed in this order, form a range of greys from black to white. Try this:

```
10    FOR X = 0 TO 7
20    PRINT INK X; "■■"
      (two solid squares obtained by pressing the white shift key,
      followed by key "9" and then key "8")
30    NEXT X
```

The color codes also relate to how the colors are produced by the television. A color TV uses blue, green and red light. All other colors can be made up of a mixture of these three. Magenta is made by mixing blue and red and its code, 3, is the sum of the other two colors' codes.

When you first switch on your Sinclair you will see that the entire screen is white and you are typing on the screen in black. It is easy to add a splash of color by using the BORDER command to be found on the B key. Try this:

```
BORDER 1      (followed by ENTER)
```

This turns the border dark blue. You can put any one of the eight numbers after the BORDER command, and after pressing ENTER the border around the screen will change to that color. You can also choose what are called INK and PAPER colors. The PAPER color is the color of the rectangular page inside the border, and the INK color is the color of the text and graphics characters that you type in. Getting the PAPER and INK commands is a little harder than the BORDER one. To change the PAPER to a new color, you first press the WHITE shift key and the symbol shift key, and lastly, still holding down the symbol shift key, you press the C key. Try some of the following (note that as with the BORDER command above, you don't need line numbers for these examples):

```
PAPER 3: CLS      (the CLS command is on the "V" key)
PAPER 2: CLS
PAPER 6: CLS
```

You see the main rectangle of the screen's page turn first magenta, then red and then yellow. As you probably know, you can put any of the eight colors' numbers after the PAPER command. But to get the color all over the page, you must then follow your PAPER command by a CLS (clear the screen) command (there is a way of avoiding this—but I'll return to that later).

The INK command is just as easy to use. To get INK you press the CAPS SHIFT key again, holding it down you press the SYMBOLS SHIFT key on the right, and still holding the red shift key down, press the X key. The INK command is used in much the same way as the PAPER one.

To see the effect of colored text try:

```
10   PAPER 7
20   INK 3
30   CLS
40   PRINT "Testing"
```

If you run this program you'll see the computer prints the text in magenta on a white background. You can put any color text on top of any color paper, but many of the colors do not mix very well. To see what I mean change the above program to the following, and run it:

```
10   PAPER 5
20   INK 4
30   CLS
40   PRINT "Testing"
```

It is very difficult to see the words. Cyan and green don't mix too well either and typing green text on top of a cyan paper is particularly difficult to read.

You can use the color commands to color just a part of the screen, rather than change the whole page within the border. To see this, try the following:

```
PAPER 7:CLS:PRINT INK 5; PAPER 1; "Testing"
```

As you can see, just the area behind the words was in light blue, with the text in dark blue.

There are four things that you can do to the color and all the BASIC words for these can be found below the bottom row of keys on your Timex Sinclair; they are FLASH, BRIGHT, OVER and INVERSE. The last two of these are not restricted to the use of color, but they have many uses when dealing with color.

BRIGHT

The BRIGHT command is easy to understand. This is used to make the color of either the text (INK) or the background (PAPER) stand out a little more. Using it the colors can be made a little brighter and in some cases a hue or so lighter. This routine shows what BRIGHT does:

```
10   FOR x=0 to 7
20   PRINT PAPERx;BRIGHT 0;" ";BRIGHT 1;" ";
30   NEXT x
```

This prints spaces (think of them as little blocks of PAPER) in blocks of two. The first is the normal color and the second is the same color made brighter. As you can see the BRIGHT command is followed by either a zero or a one. Zero turns BRIGHT off, and one turns it on.

This next program produces the same result, putting the BRIGHT control in a loop:

```
10   FOR x=0 TO 7
20   FOR y=0 TO 1
30   PRINT INK x; BRIGHT y;" ";
40   NEXT y
50   NEXT x
```

FLASH

The next word is FLASH and it is used rather like BRIGHT. It too is followed either by a zero or a one depending on whether it is "on" or "off." We could make the BRIGHTer squares in the last example flash for instance with this routine:

```
10   FOR x=0 TO 7
20   FOR y=0 TO 1
30   PRINT INK x;BRIGHT y; FLASH y;" ";
40   NEXT y: NEXT x
```

The routine shows that FLASH flashes between the color of the INK and the color of the paper. If you have just switched on then the INK is set to INK 9. INK 9 is a special statement which tells the Timex Sinclair to print in whatever INK would be the best contrast to the present PAPER color. The program you've just run shows that for the four darker colors the Timex Sinclair chooses white as the INK and the other lighter colors have black. Hence the BRIGHTened dark colored squares flash between color and white, and the lighter colors flash between color and black.

INK 8 is also a valid statement. It means that the last color is to be retained. You can use these two numbers with PAPER commands as well, and they have the same effect. Thus, PAPER 8 and PAPER 9 are valid statements. You can use the number 8 after the FLASH and BRIGHT statements, but not the 9. In all cases the number 8 means that what ever attribute that square was set to will be retained when a new character is printed on top.

INVERSE, OVER

The two remaining words that you can use when dealing with color are INVERSE and OVER. INVERSE carries out the basic action in FLASH, namely to change the INK to PAPER and the PAPER to INK. This has the effect of inverting the text, so white writing on black becomes black on white, or vice versa. It works for all the colors of INK or PAPER and takes a form similar to BRIGHT and FLASH. Once again, the word is followed by either a zero (meaning "off") or a one (meaning "on"). However you can't use 8 after this word. Try this to see how it works:

```
10   FOR x=0 TO 1
20   PRINT INVERSE x; INK 5; PAPER 1; "This shows
     how inverse works"
30   PAUSE 50
40   NEXT x
```

OVER is a very useful BASIC word and it refers to a way in which you can overlay one character on top of another. Once again it uses the zero-for-off and one-for-on control. Like INVERSE, you can't use the number 8 after it. OVER works by calculating what is called an exclusive-or operation on a character square. What this means is that it lays one character over another, but where there is a black dot in both at the same place it will print a white dot instead. The way OVER does its job is best understood by considering that each character square on the screen (there are 32 across and 24 down) is made up of 64 tiny dots in an 8 by 8 matrix (rather like a chess board or a square of graph paper). When asked to OVER print something the Timex Sinclair looks at the same dot in each of the character squares in question and goes by this "truth table" to decide whether to end up with that dot as black or white:

		New Character	
		Black Dot	*White Dot*
Old Character	*Black Dot*	*White*	*Black*
	White Dot	*Black*	*White*

Let's take an example to make this clear. Print two characters onto your TV screen, the capital "O" and the zero "0":

```
PRINT "O 0"
```

Now imagine what you would get if you OVER PRINTed the capital O on top of the zero. Having formed a mental image of what you expect (bearing in mind that two blacks give a white) now try the actual OVER PRINTing:

```
PRINT OVER 1; "O"; CHR$8; "0"
```
(Note that CHR$8 is a control character which backspaces)

You should get a cross-hatch line, or slash / . Do you see why? Try OVER PRINTing a few other characters on top of each other and try to predict what will happen.

How else can OVER PRINTing be used? One good use is making objects appear to pass in front of or behind others. A simple example of this is in the program OVERPRINT. In this a normal letter "p" travels across the screen toward an inverse "p". The normal "p" passes over the other one momentarily creating a black square (remember that black and white give black?) then goes on its way leaving the inverse "p" as it was.

OVERPRINT

```
    5 PAPER 5. INK 1. CLS
   10 PRINT INVERSE 1;AT 10,10;"p
"
   15 FOR a=0 TO 20
   20 PRINT PAPER 1; INK 5; INVER
SE 1; OVER 1;AT 10,a;"p"
   30 PAUSE 10
   40 PRINT INVERSE 1; OVER 1,AT
10,a;"p"
   50 NEXT a
```

ATTR

I mentioned that you can only have one INK color and one PAPER color in each character square. This is because the Timex Sinclair stores information about the color of INK, of PAPER, whether a character is FLASHing or not, and whether it is BRIGHT or normal, for each character square in an area of memory set aside for "attributes" (from location 22528 to 23296). This gives 768 memory locations which is 32×24, the number of columns multiplied by the number of rows on the TV screen. Each of these memory locations contains a number between 0 and 255 which refers to what colors are there and so on. This number is returned when you use the Sinclair BASIC term ATTR (x,y) where x and y are the coordinates (as in PRINT AT) of the square in question. The number is not easy to understand until you have had some practice with it.

It is made up of four numbers added together. These are:

> 128 or 0 depending on whether the square is FLASHing
> 64 or 0 depending on whether it is BRIGHT or not
> 8 times the PAPER color's code
> and lastly the code for the INK color.

You use ATTR as follows:

```
PRINT AT 10, 10; FLASH 1; BRIGHT 1; INK2;
PAPER 6; "S" ;ATTR (10, 10)
```

Here you are printing the letter S at the position row 10, column 10, in red ink on a yellow background with BRIGHT and FLASH both on. What do you think the computer will report as the ATTR of position 10, 10? It should be $128 + 64 + 8*6 + 2 = 242$. This is fairly easy to work out given that you know the attributes. If you are just given the response to ATTR (x,y), and you want to work out what the number means, you can use the "ATTR" calculator program.

You could set variable "A" equal to the result of ATTR (x,y) in a program and make use of the values of INK, PAPER, BRIGHT and FLASH obtained. One good use for ATTR is detecting the nature of the character at a certain position. For instance, you might wish to have a space craft travel along until it hits a mountain. You could set the mountain up in a different color to the rest of the picture, and by testing whether the character space ahead of the craft is that of the mountain or not you could tell when collision will occur.

ATTR CALCULATOR

```
10 INPUT "ATTR?";A
20 IF A-128<0 THEN GO TO 50
30 LET a=a-128: PRINT "Flash o
n,";
40 GO TO 60
50 PRINT "Flash off,",
60 IF a-64<0 THEN GO TO 90
70 LET A=A-64: PRINT "Bright o
n,";
80 GO TO 100
90 PRINT "Bright off,",
100 IF A/8=INT (A/8) THEN GO TO
140
120 PRINT "Paper is ";INT (A/8)
,",Ink is ";A-(8*INT (A/8))
130 STOP
140 PRINT "No Ink,Paper is ";A/
8
```

In this case the mountain will usually be in a known position (although you could arrange for a moving planet surface) so the use of ATTR is not of great value. But in other cases you will not know exactly where an "obstacle" is or you may only be able to note obstacles' positions by many IF . . . THEN statements. In these circumstances, ATTR could be very useful.

PLOTTING A RAINBOW

Let's try some high resolution printing in color. The next program plots a rainbow. Take note of how the command to draw an arc of a circle is used to produce curves of color. Note too that the arcs of a different color are a character space apart. Can you recall why this must be so? There can only be one INK color in each character space, so if you draw two differently colored lines too close together, then the color of the second one will "contaminate" the first by changing all the INK values in that square to its own code.

RAINBOW

```
1 REM RAINBOW
2 LET X=1
3 DIM a(6): GO SUB 100
4 LET y=1
5 PAPER 7: BORDER 0: CLS
```

```
  10 FOR a=160 TO 250 STEP 15
  20 FOR u=1 TO 5
  30 INK a(y): PLOT a+u,0: DRAW
-a,a-80+u,PI/2
  40 NEXT u
  50 LET y=y+1
  60 IF y=7 THEN GO TO 200
  70 NEXT a
 100 LET a(1)=3: LET a(2)=1: LET
a(3)=5: LET a(4)=4: LET a(5)=6:
LET a(6)=2
 110 RETURN
 200 PRINT PAPER 7;AT 19,5; INK
3;"S"; INK 1;"P"; INK 5;"E"; INK
 4;"CT"; INK 6;"R"; INK 2;"UM"
```

128 COLORS

Being able to print two colors in each character square can be used to
advantage to create up to 128 colors on your Timex Sinclair. You need first
to define a graphics character which looks like a very small chess board.

   By making the PAPER one color and the INK another you will effectively make half of the character one color and the other half the other.
Because the colors are spread evenly, the two colors mix to form a new
one. Red dots and yellow dots mixed in this way, for example, give a good
orange. Try it now, and see just how many different colors can be produced on the Timex Sinclair with the program.

COLORS

```
  10 REM COLORS
  20 PAPER 7: BORDER 6: CLS
  30 REM CHESS-BOARD LIKE CHR$
  40 FOR X=0 TO 6 STEP 2
  50 POKE USR "P"+X,85
  60 POKE USR "P"+X+1,170
  70 NEXT X
  80 FOR P=0 TO 7
  90 FOR I=0 TO 7
 100 FOR B=0 TO 1
 110 PRINT PAPER P; INK I; BRIGH
T B;"PP";
 120 NEXT B: NEXT I: NEXT P
 130 PAUSE 200
 140 CLS : PRINT "AND NOW FULL S
CREEN...": PAUSE 200
 150 CLS
 160 POKE 23692,100
 170 FOR P=0 TO 7
 180 FOR I=0 TO 7
 190 FOR B=0 TO 1
 200 FOR K=0 TO 31
 210 PRINT PAPER P; INK I; BRIGH
T B;"PPPPPPPPPPPPPPPPPPPPPPPPPPPP
PPPPP"
```

```
220 REM ALL  'P'S ARE GRAPHICS
    CHR$ ON KEY 'P'
230 NEXT K
240 POKE 23692,100:
    REM AUTO SCROLL
250 NEXT B: NEXT I: NEXT P
260 STOP
```

You could do this another way by drawing cross-hatched lines across the screen using the DRAW and PLOT commands, drawing the lines so that they are one pixel (dot) apart. By drawing in one INK on top of a different colored paper the same effect could be obtained as when the graphics character was used.

The Timex Sinclair can produce a very fine display by drawing lines with the DRAW command which interact to give a kind of "interference pattern." NETWORK is a good demonstration of this.

This program plots the screen's central position over and over again each time drawing from that point to a position on the edge of the screen. If you draw to every edge position you will eventually get a solid mass of color. But by drawing to pixels at least one pixel apart very interesting patterns emerge. This is because the lines your Timex Sinclair draws are not completely straight, but vary in fixed ways depending to what point and from what point they are drawn. The program draws all INK colors against all possible different PAPER colors, and the effect depends on the color mix involved. Some colors seem to interfere with each other more than others, and others appear to swim around the screen in eddies caused by the pattern.

NETWORK

```
10 REM NETWORK
20 LET Z=1
30 LET ink=(RND*5)+1
40 LET paper=(RND*5)+1
50 IF ink=paper THEN GO TO 30
55 PAPER paper: INK ink: CLS
60 FOR A=1 TO 2
70 FOR X=0 TO 254 STEP 2
80 PLOT 128,88: DRAW (-127*Z)+
(X*Z),Z*-87
90 NEXT X
100 FOR Y=0 TO 175 STEP 2
110 PLOT 128,88: DRAW 127*Z,Z*-
87+(Y*Z)
120 NEXT Y
130 LET Z=-Z
140 NEXT A: PAUSE 100: GO TO 20
```

The next program is at least as attractive as NETWORK. I've called it ICESTAR. It draws a many-armed star in white and then, using a technique which adds a new dimension to your Timex Sinclair, overlays a new

PAPER color on top of (or underneath) the snowflake. Usually, as you'll recall, to change the PAPER color you need to first state the color number, and then use the CLS (clear screen) command. Of course, this destroys the pattern you've drawn. For this reason, in this program, the Timex Sinclair creates a string of spaces the same length as the size of the screen (704 character positions) and by printing this string over the pattern in random colors, a splendid effect is obtained.

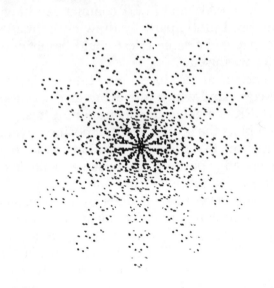

ICESTAR

```
 10 REM ICESTAR
 20 INK 7: BORDER 3: PAPER 1: C.
LS
 30 LET P$=" ": LET T$=" "
 40 FOR X=0 TO 702
 50 LET P$=P$+T$
 60 PRINT "."; : NEXT X
 70 REM CREATED STRING OF
       SPACES SIZE OF SCREEN
 80 CLS
 90 LET FLAG=0
100 FOR K=20 TO 80 STEP 12
110 LET Y=0: LET Z=PI
120 LET C=100
130 LET E=(Z-Y)/C
140 FOR L=Y TO Z STEP E
150 LET S=K*COS (L*6)
160 LET H=S*SIN L
170 LET V=S*COS L
180 PLOT 128+H,88+V
190 NEXT L
200 LET FLAG=FLAG+1
210 IF  FLAG=101 THEN GO TO 230
220 GO TO 150
230 LET FLAG=0: NEXT K
```

```
240 LET COL=INT (RND*6)+1
250 PRINT AT 0,0; PAPER COL; OV
ER 1;P$
260 PAUSE 100: GO TO 240
```

You can achieve this same result in another way too. Think how? The most obvious alternative is to POKE the ATTRibute area of memory with the code to change the PAPER color of each location on the screen. The ATTRibute area begins at 22528 and the screen on which PAPER is changed (excluding the bottom two lines where new program lines are entered) ends at 23231. The following program also changes the color of the screen without destroying the text or pattern there:

```
10   FOR x = 22528 TO 23231
20   POKE x,32
30   NEXT x
```

Can you see which color I'm POKEing? Keeping in mind that the PAPER color is stored as eight times its code, this has POKEd the screen with code 4, which is green.

The next program, NIGHTWATCH, plots a very attractive, balanced picture on the screen, using many of the color commands we've discussed so far in this chapter.

NIGHTWATCH

```
10 REM NIGHTWATCH
20 PAPER 0: INK 7: BORDER 0: C
LS
30 LET A=INT (127*RND)
40 LET B=INT (87*RND)
50 LET Z=INT (8*RND)
60 LET R=INT (RND*6)
70 IF R<2.5 THEN GO TO 140
80 INK Z
90 PLOT 127-A,87+B
100 PLOT 127+A,87-B
110 PLOT 127-A,87-B
120 PLOT 127+A,87+B
130 GO TO 30
140 PLOT OVER 1; 127-A,87-B
150 PLOT OVER 1; 127+A,87+B
160 PLOT OVER 1; 127-A,87+B
170 PLOT OVER 1; 127+A,87-B
180 GO TO 30
```

Drawing circles in color on your Spectrum can be rewarding. The statement you use is of the form: CIRCLE INK i;x,y,z where *i* is the INK color, *x* and *y* are the coordinates of the center of the circle, and *z* its radius. RANDOM CIRCLES is a program which, as its name suggests, draws randomly-placed circles in randomly-chosen colors.

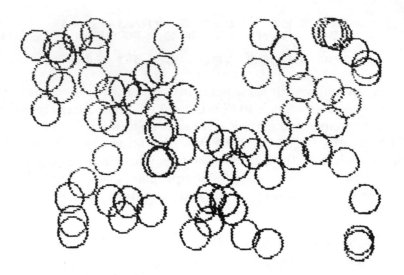

RANDOM CIRCLES

```
  1 REM    RANDOM CIRCLES
  5 PAPER 0: CLS
 10 LET X=(234*RND)+10
 20 LET Y=(154*RND)+10
 30 LET Z=(5*RND)+1
 40 CIRCLE INK Z;X,Y,10
 50 GO TO 10
```

The BOWLING BALL program does its work by drawing circles of increasing radii from the same center (using a STEP of 0.1 in the radius increase). This has the strange effect of leaving five main white areas in the balls, and hence the name for the program.

BOWLING BALL

```
  5 INK 1: PAPER 6: CLS
 10 LET X=100: LET Y=X
 20 FOR a=0 TO 22 STEP .1
 30 CIRCLE X,Y,a
 40 NEXT a
 50 LET X=130: LET Y=85
 60 GO TO 20
```

Drawing circles one on top of another, as you saw in the random circles program above, can produce multi-colored circles, because as two circles are printed close together, the color of the second changes part of that of the first. This effect is used again in the program CONE.

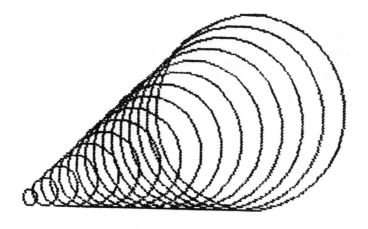

CONE

```
  1 REM     CONE
 10 BORDER 6
 20 PAPER 0:  CLS
 30 LET Y=30
 40 FOR X=30 TO 180 STEP 10
 50 LET Z=(6*RND)+1
 60 CIRCLE INK Z;X,Y,Y-25
 70 LET Y=Y+4
 80 NEXT X
 90 PAUSE 0
```

As you can see the circles are drawn in ever-increasing size and in random colors, producing an almost three-dimensional effect.

The final program could form the basis of a rather more complex figure drawing and coloring program. It allows you to draw a triangle of any size within the screen's boundaries and it will be filled in the color of your choice.

TRIANGLE DRAWER

```
  1 REM TRIANGLE DRAWER
  5 BORDER 1: PAPER 7: CLS
 10 INPUT "START X COORDINATE";
X
 20 INPUT "START Y COORDINATE?"
;Y
 30 INPUT "HEIGHT?";H
 35 IF Y+H>175 THEN GO TO 100
 40 INPUT "LENGTH?";L
 45 IF X+L>255 THEN GO TO 100
 50 INPUT "COLOUR?";C
 55 CLS
 60 FOR P=0 TO H
```

```
 70 PLOT X,Y: DRAW INK C;L,P
 80 NEXT P
 90 STOP
100 CLS : PRINT "OUT OF RANGE"'
'"ENTER AGAIN"
110 GO TO 10
```

3
■

Exploring the Timex Sinclair's Sound

As you probably know, it is very easy to get sounds out of your Timex Sinclair. You use the BEEP command. (You'll find it printed on your keyboard in black below the Z key. First press the white CAPS SHIFT key, and the SYMBOL SHIFT key on the right-hand side at the same time, and finally—still holding down the black shift key—press the "Z" key.) To make a sound, type in something like this: BEEP 1,0 (followed by ENTER). If you try this you'll hear a tone which is about a second long and at a pitch around middle C. The first number refers to how long a note is wanted, and the second determines the note's pitch. The "duration" number, which can be from about 0.00125 to around 10, is in seconds. Any time shorter than 0.00125 will not really sound at all, and a duration longer than 10 seconds will throw up an error report, "Integer out of range".

The second number can be in the range −60 to + 69. Each step refers to either a semitone above middle C (which is number 0) or a semitone below it. So BEEP 1,1 will sound a tone a semitone above middle C for a second, and BEEP 1,−10 will sound a note 10 semitones below middle C. Remember to put the comma between the two numbers.

You can get some idea of the range of frequencies the Timex Sinclair can produce by running the following short program:

```
10   FOR n = -60 TO 69
20   BEEP .2,n
30   NEXT n
```

29

As you heard, the pitches ranged from a series of fast clicks to high warbles. For music you may well conclude, as I have, that the most useful range is around middle C—about ±20 either side—and this possibly explains Sinclair's assignment of middle C to zero. However, the highest and lowest pitches can be of use as well, as we'll see in due course.

You have probably noticed how quiet the sound is. To get louder sound, you need a lead to plug your Timex Sinclair into an external amplifier. Most amplifiers with a "mic" socket are suitable. You can get the sound signal from both the "ear" and the "mic" sockets at the back of the Timex Sinclair, with the "ear" signal being a little stronger. You may have to experiment to see which is best to attach to your amplifier.

Once you attach an external amplifier you may notice that as you press each key there is a click. This feedback on pressing a key can be useful, but the click you hear without external amplification is much too quiet to be of use. You can remedy this by entering the following, as a direct command: POKE 23609, 100 (then press ENTER).

Now, whenever you press a key there is a distinct beep. This can be very useful when you're typing quickly, and only looking at the screen occasionally. However this beep will also be amplified by your external amplifier when you use one. You will either have to put up with this or leave your Timex Sinclair in its "click" state whenever you are using sound a lot. Of course you can plug and unplug the leads at the back, but this is rather a lot of fuss. If you do use an external amplifier, though, you will have to unplug the amplifier from the back of your Timex Sinclair each time you want to load a program or save one (depending on which outlet you used at the back).

Let's get back now to the music. As each note number in the BEEP command represents a semitone rise (or fall if it's a negative number), there are 12 of these to an octave. Thus middle C is 0, and the C above is 12, and so on. You could type music into your Timex Sinclair by setting your tune out as notes on staves, with bar lines, and then convert each note to its BEEP number and each note's duration to a number (probably setting a single beat as 0.25 seconds). But this is time-consuming. It would be much more convenient to be able to type in a melody as a series of letters for notes, and numbers for beats.

Our MUSIC PLAYER Program allows you to do this. It tells you it treats the letters A to G as the lower octave (where "C" is middle C) and letters a to c as the next higher octave. You enter your melody as a single line where each note is followed by a number which indicates its duration. I've chosen 1 to represent a one beat note, 2 for two beats and so forth. To give yourself a choice of speed add a line like this:

```
5     INPUT "What speed? 1 is slow, 5 is fast";x
```

You also need to change line 370 where the BEEP command is executed:

```
370    BEEP X(Z)/X,Y(Z)
```

As you'll see when you try this program, it is much easier than having to write out music on staves beforehand.

MUSIC PLAYER

```
10 REM MUSIC PLAYER
20 DIM X(50): DIM Y(50)
30 LET K=0: LET L=1
40 BORDER 2: PAPER 4: INK 9: CLS
50 PRINT AT 0,10; INVERSE 1;"MUSIC PLAYER"''
60 PRINT "TYPE IN YOUR MUSIC AS A LINE OF LETTERS AND NUMBERS."
70 PRINT ''"PUT NOTES AS LETTERS FOLLOWED BY THEIR LENGTH IN BEATS"
80 PRINT ''"YOU  HAVE TWO OCTAVES.THE LOWER ONE IS FROM A TO G AND THE UPPER FROM a TO c."
90 INPUT N$
100 FOR A=1 TO LEN N$ STEP 2
110 IF CODE N$(A)<97 THEN GO TO 280
120 IF N$(A)="a" THEN LET K=-0.5
130 IF N$(A)="d" THEN LET K=0.5
140 IF N$(A)="e" THEN LET K=1
150 IF N$(A)="f" THEN LET K=1
160 IF N$(A)="g" THEN LET K=1.5
170 LET Y(L)=(CODE N$(A)-87)+(2*K)
180 LET L=L+1
190 LET K=0
200 NEXT A
210 LET L=1
220 FOR T=2 TO LEN N$ STEP 2
230 LET X(L)=VAL N$(T)/2
240 LET L=L+1
250 NEXT T
260 GO TO 360
270 STOP
280 IF N$(A)="A" THEN LET K=-0.5
290 IF N$(A)="B" THEN LET K=-0.5
300 IF N$(A)="F" THEN LET K=0.5
310 IF N$(A)="G" THEN LET K=0.5
320 LET Y(L)=(CODE N$(A)-67-K)*2
330 LET K=0
340 LET L=L+1
350 GO TO 200
360 FOR Z=1 TO LEN N$/2
370 BEEP X(Z)/2,Y(Z)
380 NEXT Z
```

PIANO

It would be good to be able to play the Timex Sinclair as a piano. The next program allows you to do this. It uses the INKEY$ command to scan the keyboard to see which key you press. I've written it so that you have a choice of three octaves with the note "C" being on the "T" key in each case. A pictorial version of your "piano" keyboard is presented on the screen to help you remember which keys go with which notes. You can think of the letters Q to P as the white piano keys and the numbers above them as black sharps and flats. The Timex Sinclair was designed to play a fairly good "even tempered" scale, which is rather like that on a real piano, so you should get reasonable (if rather quiet) music from your "piano."

PIANO

```
  10 REM PIANO
  20 INK 7: BORDER 0: PAPER 2: C
LS
  30 PRINT AT 5,12; INVERSE 1; "P
IANO"
  40 PRINT AT 8,0; "YOUR    PIANO'S
    WHITE   KEYS   ARE         THOSE F
ROM 'Q' TO 'P'"
  50 PRINT AT 12,0; "PRESSING 'Z'
   WILL GIVE A HIGHER OCTAVE, 'X'
GIVES A LOWER ONE"
  60 PRINT AT 16,0; INVERSE 1; "P
RESS 'V' FOR VIBRATO AND 'M' TO
        SWITCH IT OFF"
  70 PRINT AT 19,0; INVERSE 1; "P
RESSING 'C' PUTS  MID C ON 'T' A
GAIN"
  80 LET K=0: LET X=0.3
  90 PAUSE 500
 100 REM VISUAL DISPLAY
 110 CLS
 120 PRINT ; INVERSE 1; AT 10,4; "
Q"; AT 10,6; "W"; AT 10,8; "E"; AT 10
,10; "R"; AT 10,12; "T"; AT 10,14; "Y
"; AT 10,16; "U"; AT 10,18; "I"; AT 1
0,20; "O"; AT 10,22; "P"
 130 PRINT PAPER 0; AT 8,5; "2"; AT
8,7; "3"; AT 8,9; "4"; AT 8,13; "6";
AT 8,15; "7"; AT 8,19; "9"; AT 8,21;
"0"
 140 IF INKEY$="Z" THEN LET K=12
 150 IF INKEY$="X" THEN LET K=-1
2
 160 IF INKEY$="C" THEN LET K=0
 170 IF INKEY$="V" THEN LET X=0.
03
 180 IF INKEY$="M" THEN LET X=0.
3
 190 IF INKEY$="2" THEN BEEP X,-
6+K
 200 IF INKEY$="3" THEN BEEP X,-
4+K
 210 IF INKEY$="4" THEN BEEP X,-
2+K
```

```
 220  IF  INKEY$="6"  THEN  BEEP  X,1
+K
 230  IF  INKEY$="7"  THEN  BEEP  X,3
+K
 240  IF  INKEY$="9"  THEN  BEEP  X,6
+K
 250  IF  INKEY$="0"  THEN  BEEP  X,8
+K
 260  IF  INKEY$="Q"  THEN  BEEP  X,-
7+K
 270  IF  INKEY$="W"  THEN  BEEP  X,-
5+K
 280  IF  INKEY$="E"  THEN  BEEP  X,-
3+K
 290  IF  INKEY$="R"  THEN  BEEP  X,-
1+K
 300  IF  INKEY$="T"  THEN  BEEP  X,0
+K
 310  IF  INKEY$="Y"  THEN  BEEP  X,2
+K
 320  IF  INKEY$="U"  THEN  BEEP  X,4
+K
 330  IF  INKEY$="I"  THEN  BEEP  X,5
+K
 340  IF  INKEY$="O"  THEN  BEEP  X,7
+K
 350  IF  INKEY$="P"  THEN  BEEP  X,9
+K
 360  GO  TO  130
 370  STOP
```

The program asks you which octave you want with a choice of either having middle C on the T key, or the octave below this or the one above. Of course, there's nothing to stop you rewriting line 140 to 350 so that touching other keys produces different notes.

Finally, the program asks you if you want "vibrato." This sets the note's duration to 0.03 seconds instead of 0.3. Experiment with other duration values to see the effect. I found that durations much longer than about half a second made it too slow to play, and much shorter than three hundredths of a second was too "clicky." You may like to think of a way to introduce a change in tempo. You'll need to have the duration of each note vary to produce variants like "slow,quick,quick." Try a subroutine with a GO SUB command. This would need to do something like play the pressed note at the basic duration and then follow it with two more notes half or even a quarter as long as the first. But don't forget that subroutines take a little time to execute, so the whole program might start to feel rather unresponsive if you add too many things.

The Timex Sinclair will allow not only fractional durations, but fractional note values as well. This might come in useful if you want to tune your "Timex Sinclair organ" to another instrument. This would be easy to do. If you add the lines:

```
 355   IF  INKEY$ = "K"  THEN  LET  K=K+0.05
 356   IF  INKEY$ = "L"  THEN  LET  K=K-0.05
```

then the notes you play will be a fraction sharper or flatter with each press of either the K or L keys (K to sharpen, L to flatten). You could use this facility of producing fractional note pitches to play "oriental" sounding music, with 16 or more notes in a scale, instead of the usual 12.

OTHER EFFECTS

You can do more with your Timex Sinclair than just turn it into a piano. A visual display of musical notes can be produced. To do this we'll use the Timex Sinclair's ability to define new characters discussed in detail in the games chapter. The MUSIC WRITER program forms the basis of a longer program which allows you to type in your music much as you did in MUSIC PLAYER as letters, numbers and # signs, but this time it turns each note into a quarter note, eighth note, or the like on the screen, printing it on the correct stave. You can change this program so that as you play your Timex Sinclair like an organ or piano, it prints the notes on the screen.

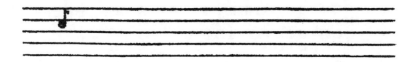

MUSIC WRITER

```
  10 REM MUSIC WRITER
  20 PAPER 6: INK 0: BORDER 7: C
LS
  30 LET X=151
  40 REM DRAW STAVES
  50 FOR Y=1 TO 5
  60 PLOT 0,X: DRAW 255,0
  70 LET X=X-8
  80 NEXT Y
  90 FOR A=0 TO 7
 100 READ T
 110 POKE USR "L"+A,T
 120 NEXT A
 130 FOR B=0 TO 7
 140 READ T
 150 POKE USR "K"+B,T
 160 NEXT B
 170 PRINT OVER 1;AT 3,3;"L";AT
4,3;"K"
 180 BEEP 0.25,0
 190 REM TOP OF NOTE SHAPE
 200 DATA 0,4,7,5,4,4,4,4
 210 REM BOTTOM OF NOTE SHAPE
 220 DATA 0,60,124,124,124,56,0,
0
 230 STOP
```

ADDING SOUND EFFECTS

There's a good chance that you are interested in playing games on your Timex Sinclair. Can the computer give the added dimension of sound to games? Can it make sounds like phasors firing, footsteps or train noises? The answer is both Yes and No. It can produce some fairly useful noises which will enhance your games.

However, if you expect the sounds to be as good as those produced by arcade machines, I'm afraid you'll be a little disappointed.

PHASOR FIRE, PHASOR FIRE 2 and PHASOR 3 give three ways of making a suitable sound for a space shooting game, and WALKING shows how you can incorporate sound with movement. Note that the first graphics character in line 140 is an L, the second is a K.

PHASOR FIRE

```
10 REM PHASOR FIRE
20 LET D=0.0125
30 FOR X=1 TO 2
40 FOR Y=4 TO 16 STEP 2
50 BEEP D,Y
60 NEXT Y
70 NEXT X
```

```
10 REM PHASOR FIRE 2
20 FOR X=-10 TO 0
30 BEEP 0.0125,X
40 NEXT X
50 FOR Y=0 TO -5 STEP -1
60 BEEP 0.0125,Y
70 NEXT Y
```

```
10 REM PHASOR 3
20 FOR X=5 TO 20 STEP 1.5
30 BEEP .008,X
40 NEXT X
50 FOR Y=20 TO 5 STEP -1.5
60 BEEP .008,Y
70 NEXT Y
80 PAUSE 30
90 RUN
```

```
10 REM WALKING
20 FOR A=0 TO 7
30 READ X
40 POKE USR "L"+A,X
50 NEXT A
60 FOR A=0 TO 7
70 READ X
80 POKE USR "K"+A,X
90 NEXT A
```

```
100 FOR T=0 TO 31
110 PRINT AT 21,T;"~";
120 NEXT T
130 FOR C=0 TO 31
140 PRINT AT 20,C;"*": PAUSE 3:
PRINT AT 20,C;"*": PAUSE 3: PRI
NT AT 20,C;" "
150 BEEP 0.02,30: BEEP 0.02,40
160 NEXT C
170 GO TO 100
180 REM DATA FOR 2 VERSIONS OF
MAN
190 DATA 24,36,153,126,24,100,1
32,4,24,36,153,126,24,38,33,32
200 STOP
```

Another useful routine is the program which simulates a bomb drop. This makes the frequency of the note fall from around the highest pitch available to one some 20 semitones lower. The rate of fall is fast at first, but gets even faster to give the impression of the bomb speeding up as it gets closer to the ground.

BOMB

```
10 REM BOMB
20 FOR X=69 TO 55 STEP -0.3
30 BEEP 0.05,X
40 NEXT X
50 FOR Y=0 TO 20
60 BEEP 0.01,-10: BEEP 0.01,-5
0: BEEP 0.01,-60
70 NEXT Y
```

The final program in this chapter, MUSIGRAPH, links together the Times Sinclair's sound and color capabilities. It sounds notes of random pitch and duration (with fixed limits). The higher the note the higher up the screen a blob of color is printed, and the longer the note, the further to the right the blob is printed. The result is a collage of color in which what you see corresponds to what you hear.

MUSIGRAPH

```
10 REM MUSIGRAPH
20 BORDER 0: PAPER 0: CLS
30 FOR X=0 TO 31
40 LET NOTE=RND*20
50 LET DUR=RND*0.4
60 LET INK=(RND*6)+1
70 PRINT INK INK;AT 20-NOTE,X;
"■"
80 BEEP DUR,NOTE
90 NEXT X
100 CLS : GO TO 30
```

4
■

Using the Timex Sinclair in Business

Like all computers, the Timex Sinclair by itself can do nothing. With appropriate software a vast variety of tasks can be handled. Users regularly buy software with many features they do not want, but which do the basic work to be done.

As time goes on (if the system is good) they gradually come to use the features, and before long they cannot understand how they got along without them. Some examples of what a computer system can do are given shortly. These examples show that computer systems can be an enormous help—if they are organized properly.

As I pointed out in the first chapter, computers can do anything which can be reduced to a set of elementary commands which they can act upon. They will always act exactly in accord with the information they've been given. For example, if your invoicing program contains a section to "send a reminder to everyone who has not paid their account this month," some people will be getting letters threatening legal action if they don't pay $0.00 at ONCE.

The degree of care required in producing and using computer programs depends upon the application. The effort required to ensure absolutely that the space shuttle goes up, rather than down, would be wasted on a new and better anagram game.

Computer applications can be grouped into a number of (not clearly delimited) classifications:

Business and Data Processing: Usually fairly simple operations are carried out on relatively large amounts of data. Stock control, for example, requires virtually nothing more difficult than addition and subtraction, but it is important to find the required data as fast as possible. Most of the time taken to run a program is used up in handling information held in memory. A well-designed business system will comprise modules which can interact with each other. That is, a sale should cause changes in your ledgers and your stock, and invoices, advice notes, and the like should be produced. There are advantages to having your word processor program interact with your business programs. Everything should be as foolproof as possible. In particular, human error should be expected and checked for when this is feasible (for example, the program should check that entries are, in some sense, reasonable). Such business systems are few and far between, but they are worth paying for.

Word Processing: The Timex Sinclair is capable of being a very respectable word processor. A word processor allows you to type in text and see it on the screen in raw form. You can edit, insert, delete or move text to your heart's delight. When the wording is right, you can print your text, neatly formatted. Then you can go back and make further changes.

Scientific or "Number-Crunching": Calculations can be very complex. Relatively little input, output, and memory may be required, but much CPU time is spent on actual calculations.

Technical Applications: The Timex Sinclair can be used to simplify life for such people as architects, planners and engineers. Elementary programming skill can pay off for these applications, as many non-standard calculations arise. Standard technical software also exists, and is often very worthwhile.

Real-Time and Control Applications: In this group, the computer is plugged into the real world. The result of a process is not a printout, but an action, such as switching motors on and off. In many cases the programs are time-critical, that is, the result must be ready at exactly the right time, neither too early nor too late. This is unlike most other applications which can proceed at their own rate.

Communications: Computers can be used to communicate with a variety of devices, including, in particular, other computers. This can be done over ordinary telephone lines. Many interesting possibilities arise.

The Timex Sinclair is well-suited to business applications because it is a powerful machine at a very reasonable price. If a business is to use a computer, there are obvious and real advantages to owning one. Just about everybody who has used a typewriter has uses for a word processor. The Timex Sinclair may emerge as a much-used real-time controller, and will show its capabilities doing useful scientific work.

It is generally recommended, quite rightly, that you should look at the software you need before deciding which computer to buy. Many people have been trapped by buying computers with impressive specifications only to discover that suitable software was not available, and would be somewhat expensive to have produced to order. This attitude should perhaps be modified slightly in view of the enormous market which the Timex Sinclair has. Whatever you need is either available now, or will probably become available in due course. Timex Sinclair business software tends to be fairly cheap compared to similar software for other machines. However, lengthy demonstrations, after-sales support, and custom modifications are rare. When selecting software for the Timex Sinclair, keep in mind that the quality of packaging and advertising will not necessarily correlate with the quality of the software. Recommendations from knowledgable users and, to a certain extent, magazine reviews are the main sources of information.

Even if you decide not to buy commercial business software at the moment, there are a number of ways you can use the computer to help you using programs you've written or adapted yourself.

The balance of this chapter is five programs I've written to give you an indication of the ways in which the Timex Sinclair can help you in a small business or at home. The programs may not fit your current needs exactly, but should be fairly easy to modify to make them suitable for you. The programs are:

Personal Accounts: allows you to specify any number of recurrent costs and—like the other programs—contains a menu to allow you, among other options, to save the current state of your accounts on tape.

Diary: sorts entries into date order, and prints them out on demand.

Telephone Directory: accepts names and telephone numbers (as might be expected), searches rapidly through the directory for a requested name and can be updated and expanded at any time.

Database: stores up to 130 items of 24 characters twice (on a 16K machine; a much larger file can be created on a 48K machine), in a way which allows them to be accessed by one of two criteria. The program is set up to store a collection of 130 records and can print out a list of records in alphabetical order by artist name or by title, and allows searches to be made through either list. It can easily be adapted to handle other requirements, and, if only a single file is required, and fewer characters per file are needed, can handle many more items, while still retaining the order and search facilities.

Financial Model/Sales Projection: one of the most popular packages of business software in the world is Visicalc, a spread sheet calculator which allows the user to feed in current figures, then make future projections based on those figures. This program performs two of the tasks of Visicalc: it analyzes the pattern of sales figures from month to month (or between whichever time periods you decide), and then allows those figures to be projected, with the projection based either on the average sale per month for the period when results are known, or on the sales results of the last known month.

These programs may well need modification to be of use to you in a small business, or for home use. The main reason for including them in this chapter, apart from their immediate use, is to show the ways business software can be written. Business software rarely contains "clever" coding as do many arcade games programs. The approach is usually more methodical and less exciting. The tasks to be accomplished by a business software package can usually be clearly delineated before you begin, whereas a game may evolve as the program is written.

You'll find it relatively easy, once you know what you're trying to achieve with a business program, to write the program, or to get someone to write it for you.

We'll now look at the programs one by one, and see what we can learn about writing business applications software from the listings.

PERSONAL ACCOUNTS

When you first run this, you'll see a menu appear which reads as follows:

```
Current balance is $0

ENTER
1 - To start from scratch
2 - To modify payment schedule
3 - To deposit money
4 - To save on tape
5 - To stop
```

It is a good idea to provide a menu like this to ensure that the program can be used without either elaborate instructions or the programmer leaning over the shoulder of the user explaining what to do next. It would be reasonable to assume that the first time you run this program, you enter

1, "To start from scratch." When you do this, you'll see: "Enter the number of items which must be paid for each month." Here you input the number of recurrent costs you have, such as your mortgage, car payment, any installment payment commitments, your credit card, other standing orders, and the like. It is best to be overgenerous with the number of categories when you first run this, as it is impossible to add later ones once you've started using the package.

If you enter 4, as the number of recurrent costs (as is shown in the sample run which follows the program listing), you'll then be asked to enter, one by one, the "name of item," and then the monthly cost of this. Names of items, and their costs, can easily be changed later on. Once you've run through the list (adding "blank" items for spare numbers you've given yourself in excess of your immediate needs), you'll be given the chance to modify any of them you wish: "If this is correct, press ENTER. If there is an error, enter the number of the item you wish to change."

If the program does not yet have your bank balance, as it will not when you first run it, it will instruct you to "Enter last known balance," and then "Enter any deposits, including salary, one by one. Terminate entries by entering "E" ". As you enter any deposits you've made, the balance figure—shown at the top left hand corner of the screen—will automatically increase. Once you've added all your deposits, and signaled this to the Timex Sinclair by entering "E", you'll be given a further choice: "Enter 1 to subtract all of current payment schedule, or 2 for menu". If you enter 1, the computer will subtract the total cost of all the items you listed earlier as your recurrent costs. It will print up the balance before, and after, the month's costs have been subtracted.

You will then be back at the starting menu, by this time the "Current balance figure is . . ." is not (we hope) zero, as it was the first time you ran the program. All variables within a program are saved with the program when it is saved on cassette. However, starting the program next time with RUN or CLEAR will wipe out the contents. The last line of the program (GO TO 430) ensures that, after the first time you use the program, it will start running automatically, retaining your present balance.

Notice, when you run this program, the use of INK and FLASH to highlight parts of the program. The color and other graphic effects should be used whenever necessary to cut down on the possibility of operator error. As well as this, input should be "error-trapped" where possible, so that a user error does not cause the whole program to crash. For example, line 325 rejects a null input from line 320. A null input (just pressing ENTER without previously entering a number) would cause a crash at line 340. Similarly, although the program asks (in line 310) for "E" to be entered to terminate the entry of deposits, the program will also accept "e" as there are no instructions within the program to ensure that CAPS LOCK has been engaged.

PERSONAL ACCOUNTS

```
  10 REM PERSONAL ACCOUNTS
  12 LET BALANCE=0
  15 GO TO 430
  20 PRINT ''"Enter the number
of items which must be paid for
each month"
  30 INPUT NUMBER: CLS
  40 DIM A$(NUMBER,12)
  50 DIM A(NUMBER)
  60 FOR A=1 TO NUMBER
  70 PRINT AT A-1,0;"Enter name
of item "; FLASH 1;A
  80 INPUT A$(A)
  90 PRINT AT A-1,0;"And how muc
h is ";A$(A),"each month? (in $)
"
 100 INPUT A(A)
 110 PRINT AT A-1,0;A;TAB 3;A$(A
);TAB 15;"$";A(A);"
                                 "
 120 NEXT A
 130 PRINT '"If this is correct,
 press", FLASH 1;"ENTER"; FLASH
0;". If there is an error,","ent
er the number of the item","you
wish to change."
 140 INPUT B$
 150 IF B$="" THEN GO TO 260
 160 LET B=VAL B$
 170 PRINT "Enter new name for i
tem ";B
 180 INPUT A$(B)
 190 PRINT "And how much is ",A$
(B),," each month? (in $)"
 200 INPUT A(B)
 210 CLS
 220 FOR A=1 TO NUMBER
 230 PRINT A;TAB 3;A$(A);TAB 15;
"$";A(A)
 240 NEXT A
 250 GO TO 130
 260 CLS
 265 IF BALANCE<>0 THEN GO TO 29
0
 270 PRINT ''"Enter last known b
alance"
 280 INPUT BALANCE
 290 CLS
 300 PRINT AT 0,0;"$";BALANCE
 310 PRINT ''"Enter any deposits
, including","salary, one by one
.","Terminate entries by enterin
g ", FLASH 1;"E"
 320 INPUT Q$
 325 IF Q$="" THEN GO TO 320
 330 IF Q$="E" OR Q$="e" THEN GO
TO 360
 340 LET BALANCE=BALANCE+VAL Q$
 350 GO TO 300
 360 INPUT "Enter 1 to subtract
all of","current payment schedul
e","or 2 for menu";C
```

```
365 IF C=2 THEN GO TO 450
370 LET SPEND=0: FOR A=1 TO NUM
BER
380 LET SPEND=SPEND+A(A)
390 NEXT A
400 CLS
410 PRINT ''"Balance before cur
rent","costs was $";BALANCE
420 LET BALANCE=BALANCE-SPEND
430 PRINT ''"Current balance is
$";BALANCE
440 PAUSE 200
450 PRINT '"ENTER"
460 PRINT '"1 - To start from s
cratch"
470 PRINT '"2 - To modify payme
nt schedule"
480 PRINT '"3 - To deposit mone
y"
485 PRINT '"4 - To save on tape
"
490 PRINT '"5 - To stop"
500 INPUT C: CLS
510 IF C=1 THEN LET BALANCE=0:
GO TO 20
520 IF C=2 THEN GO TO 210
530 IF C=3 THEN GO TO 300
540 IF C=4 THEN SAVE "ACCOUNTS"
550 IF C=5 THEN STOP
560 GO TO 430
```

SAMPLE RUN: PERSONAL ACCOUNTS

```
ENTER

1 - To start from scratch

2 - To modify payment schedule

3 - To deposit money

4 - To save on tape

5 - To stop


1   Credit card $675.5
2   Mortgage    $765.34
3   Car         $456.23
4   Transport   $98.42

If this is correct, press
ENTER. If there is an error,
enter the number of the item
you wish to change.


$12354.64


Enter any deposits, including
salary, one by one.
Terminate entries by entering E
```

```
Balance before current
costs was $12489.29

Current balance is $10293.8
ENTER
1 - To start from scratch
2 - To modify payment schedule
3 - To deposit money
4 - To save on tape
5 - To stop
```

DIARY

The diary program can be used, of course, for any scheduling system and although it deals with days at the moment, it can be fairly easily modified to work for hours of the day if your needs so dictate.

This is a much simpler program than any of the others in this chapter because its task is fairly easy to outline: (a) accept a date and an event; (b) sort the events into date order and (c) print them out on demand.

However the program is not as simple as it could be because of the way we write dates. Although this program will only accept dates in one form, as the number of the day, a slash (/), the number of the month, slash, and the year, a moment's thought will show that if the computer just ignored the slashes, and sorted the dates by their size, it would put the 12th of December 1901 ahead of the first of January 1999 (121201 is a bigger number than 10199). Therefore the program must be able to manipulate the date in such a way as to ensure that earlier dates come out as "smaller numbers," but can still be printed in a form a human being will recognize. A further problem comes from the fact that the day can be one or two digits, and the month can be one or two digits. The computer must be able to add a leading zero to single digit months or days (and, of course, must know when such a zero is needed).

The routine which does all this lies between lines 40 and 80. Line 40 asks you to enter the date, given an example of the form required. Line 50 sets another string (A$) equal to the date, so it can be simply printed in a few lines' time. Line 60 checks to see if the second element of the date string is a slash, and if it is, knows that the month is a single digit, so adds a zero at the beginning. Line 70 checks to see if the fifth element of the date string is a slash (which it will only be if the day is a single digit) and if it is, adds a zero before the day digit. Then, in line 80, the date is rearranged so that the year comes first, followed by the month, and then the day.

Line 90 prints the date in its original form (which is why we set B$ equal to the date you entered) in the top right hand corner. You are then asked to enter the "event" you wish to record next to that date. As in the PERSONAL ACCOUNTS program, you now have the ability to accept the entry in its present form, or reject it to enter it again.

Assuming that you have accepted it, the program makes the element of the D$ array, which is holding your diary, equal to the date (in its computer-readable form) and the event.

The routine from 220 then sorts out the contents of the diary, and prints them in a form you will understand, with line 330 turning the date back into a form you will recognize. Underneath the program is a short sample run. As an exercise, you may want to add a menu—as in the PERSONAL ACCOUNTS program—to allow you to save the diary as it is or amend it. Even in its present form, if you save the diary on cassette, and then start it with GO TO 40 (rather than RUN), you'll retain all the previous diary contents, and be able to add additional ones which will automatically be sorted into date order.

DIARY

```
 10 REM DIARY
 20 DIM D$(200,32)
 30 FOR D=1 TO 200
 40 INPUT "Enter date (as 12/25
/84)  ";B$
 50 LET A$=B$
 60 IF A$(2)="/" THEN LET A$="0
"+A$
 70 IF A$(5)="/" THEN LET A$=A$
( TO 3)+"0"+A$(4 TO )
 80 LET A$=A$(7 TO 8)+A$(1 TO 2
)+A$(4 TO 5)
 90 PRINT AT 0,0;"Date: ";B$
100 PRINT ''"Enter schedule ite
m","(No more than 22 letters)"
110 INPUT C$
120 CLS
130 PRINT AT 0,0;B$;"-";C$
140 PRINT ''"If this is correct
, press ";INVERSE 1;"ENTER"; IN
VERSE 0,"If incorrect, press ";
FLASH 1;""E"";FLASH 0,"then ENT
ER"
150 INPUT E$: CLS
160 IF E$<>"" THEN GO TO 40
170 LET D$(D)=A$+C$
180 PRINT ''"Press ";INVERSE 1
;"ENTER";INVERSE 0;" to enter n
ext item,","or any letter, then
ENTER, to","print out schedule"
190 INPUT E$: CLS
200 IF E$="" THEN NEXT D
210 PRINT PAPER 2;FLASH 1;"Ple
ase stand by...": PAUSE 100: CLS

220 LET B=0
230 LET G=D
240 LET Z=1
```

```
250 LET B=Z+1
260 IF B>G THEN GO TO 330
270 IF D$(B)>D$(Z) THEN GO TO 2
90
280 LET Z=Z+1: GO TO 250
290 LET Q$=D$(Z)
300 LET D$(Z)=D$(B)
310 LET D$(B)=Q$
320 GO TO 280
330 PRINT D$(G)(3 TO 4);"/";D$(
G)(5 TO 6);"/";D$(G)(1 TO 2);"-"
;D$(G)(7 TO )
340 LET G=G-1
350 IF G>0 THEN GO TO 240
```

SAMPLE RUN: DIARY

```
08/16/84-CONGRESS ADDRESS

08/23/84-FRANCHISE EXPANSION

09/18/84-NEGOTIATE MERGER

09/30/84-VISIT LOCAL DISTRICT
```

TELEPHONE DIRECTORY

You should be able to see a link between DIARY, TELEPHONE DIREC-
TORY and the program which follows it, DATABASE. All three—in es-
sence—accept information from the user, sort it in some way (or ways in
the case of DATABASE) and then either print it out in order or allow it to
be searched. The structures of the three programs should give you a
number of clues as to how you can construct a filing/sorting/access program to suit your own needs.

The directory menu outlines the possibilities:

```
Enter one number:
1 - To start new directory
2 - To add new names
3 - To search for number
4 - To save directory
5 - To print directory
6 - To stop
```

In its present form, it will accept 200 entries of up to 32 characters, but
if you are happy to simply enter first names, then you can easily increase
the number of entries by changing line 20 to DIM D$(400,16). You enter

the name and then the number, and are given the chance to approve it, before it is added to the directory.

If you wish to enter a new name, you then press ENTER and are returned to line 40 for the next element of the directory.

If you wish to sort the directory into order, you press any key (except BREAK), then press ENTER. The directory is then sorted into alphabetical order, based on the first letter of the entered name (so you'll need to enter surnames first if you want the directory sorted by surname). You are now returned to the menu. If you enter 3 "To search for number," the program goes to line 500 and prints up "Enter name required". The program searches through the directory (taking a surprisingly short time to do so), and either prints up the number when it finds it (and it will only search for a name exactly the same, spaces and all, as the one you've directed it to look for), or reports "Name not found."

This program, like the PERSONAL ACCOUNTS one, allows you to save the directory on tape, and then have it run automatically (without losing its contents) on being reloaded. If you wish to start it manually, without losing the contents, start it with GO TO 360, rather than RUN.

TELEPHONE DIRECTORY

```
10 REM TELEPHONE DIRECTORY
15 GO TO 360
20 DIM D$(200,32)
30 FOR D=1 TO 200
40 INPUT "Enter name ";B$
90 PRINT AT 0,0;"Name: ";B$
110 INPUT "Enter telephone numb
er ";C$
120 CLS
130 PRINT AT 0,0;B$;"   ";C$
140 PRINT ''"If this is correct
,press "; INVERSE 1;"ENTER"; INV
ERSE 0,"If incorrect, press "; F
LASH 1;""E-"; FLASH 0,"then ENTE
R"
150 INPUT E$: CLS
160 IF E$<>"" THEN GO TO 40
170 LET D$(D)=B$+" "+C$
180 PRINT ''"Press "; INVERSE 1
;"ENTER"; INVERSE 0;" to enter n
ext item,","or any letter, then
ENTER, to","sort directory"
190 INPUT E$: CLS
200 IF E$="" THEN NEXT D
210 PRINT PAPER 2; FLASH 1;"Sor
ting..."
215 POKE 23692,0
220 LET B=0
230 LET G=D
240 LET Z=1
250 LET B=Z+1
260 IF B>G THEN GO TO 330
270 IF D$(B)>D$(Z) THEN GO TO 2
90
```

```
280 LET Z=Z+1: GO TO 250
290 LET Q$=D$(Z)
300 LET D$(Z)=D$(B)
310 LET D$(B)=Q$
320 GO TO 280
330 PRINT D$(G)
340 LET G=G-1
350 IF G>0 THEN GO TO 240
360 PRINT ''"Enter one number:"
370 PRINT '"1 - To start new di
rectory"
380 PRINT '"2 - To add new name
s"
390 PRINT '"3 - To search for n
umber"
400 PRINT '"4 - To save directo
ry"
405 PRINT '"5 - To print direct
ory"
410 PRINT '"6 - To stop"
420 INPUT B: CLS
430 IF B=1 THEN GO TO 20
440 IF B=2 THEN NEXT D
450 IF B=3 THEN GO TO 500
460 IF B=4 THEN SAVE "DIRECTORY
"
465 IF B=5 THEN FOR A=D TO 1 ST
EP -1: LPRINT D$(A): NEXT A
470 IF B=6 THEN STOP
480 GO TO 360
500 PRINT ''"Enter name require
d"
510 INPUT A$: LET F=LEN A$
520 PRINT '' FLASH 1; INK 1;"Se
arching for ";A$
530 FOR A=1 TO D
540 IF D$(A)( TO F)=A$ THEN PRI
NT ''D$(A)(F+1 TO ): GO TO 360
550 NEXT A
560 PRINT '"Name not found"
570 GO TO 360
```

SAMPLE RUN: TELEPHONE DIRECTORY

```
INKEY 111-8888
JOHN 444-7777
MAGGIE 222-2222
TIM 111-1111
URIAH 444-5555
XENON 656-6565
```

DATABASE

This program, which is really an elaborate form of TELEPHONE DIREC-
TORY, is designed here to hold a collection of musical records, and store
them in two files, one by name of artist, and one by title of musical
selection. It is included in this section because it can be used as a business

filing system. As with other menu-driven programs, the menu outlines the possibilities:

```
1 - Create new file
2 - Add new items
3 - Print out by artist name
4 - Print out by title
5 - Search for an artist
6 - Search for a title
7 - To save database on tape
8 - To stop
```

The program asks you to enter ARTIST/COMPOSER, then TITLE, then CLASSIFICATION. Classification is your own filing system reference. The program does not sort using this, but simply appends it to sorted lists, so looking for a title will produce the title, artist and classification; and looking for an artist will produce artist, title and classification. The F$ array holds the file which is sorted by artist, and the title file is held in the E$ array. When searching for an artist or a title, the program only compares the first four letters of the name. The printout shows a tiny DATABASE of five records, printed out in artist order, and then in title order.

DATABASE

```
  10 REM DATABASE
  20 PRINT '''"Select an option
"
  25 PRINT '"1 - Create new file
"
  30 PRINT '"2 - Add new items"
  40 PRINT '"3 - Print out by a:
tist name"
  50 PRINT '"4 - Print out by ti
tle"
  60 PRINT '"5 - Search for an a
rtist"
  70 PRINT '"6 - Search for a ti
tle"
  80 PRINT '"7 - To save databas
e on tape"
  90 PRINT '"8 - To stop"
 100 INPUT A
 110 CLS
 120 IF A=1 THEN GO SUB 210
 130 IF A=2 THEN NEXT J
 140 IF A=3 THEN GO SUB 630
 150 IF A=4 THEN GO SUB 670
 160 IF A=5 THEN GO SUB 710
 170 IF A=6 THEN GO SUB 800
 180 IF A=7 THEN SAVE "DATA"
 190 IF A=8 THEN STOP
 200 GO TO 20
 210 DIM F$(130,24): DIM E$(130,
24)
```

```
220 POKE 23692,0
230 FOR J=1 TO 130: CLS
240 PRINT AT 0,0; INK 2;"Enter
"Z" to terminate","new entries"
250 PRINT AT 10,10;"Item numbe
"; FLASH 1;J
260 INPUT "Enter artist/compose
r ";A$
270 IF A$="Z" THEN GO TO 390
280 PRINT 'A$
290 INPUT "Enter title ";T$
300 PRINT 'T$
310 INPUT "Enter classification
code ";C$
320 PRINT 'C$
330 PRINT '"If this is correct,
press "; INVERSE 1;"ENTER"; INV
ERSE 0,"if not, press any key,".
"then ENTER"
340 INPUT Z$
350 IF Z$<>"" THEN GO TO 240
360 LET F$(J)=A$+": "+T$+": "+C$
370 LET E$(J)=T$+": "+A$+": "+C$
380 NEXT J
390 CLS
400 PRINT INK 1; FLASH 1;"Pleas
e stand by...sorting      "
405 LET G=J: LET B=0
410 LET Z=1
440 LET B=Z+1
450 IF B>G THEN LET G=G-1: IF G
>0 THEN GO TO 410
455 IF G=0 THEN GO TO 520
460 IF F$(B)<F$(Z) THEN GO TO 4
80
470 LET Z=Z+1: GO TO 440
480 LET Q$=F$(Z)
490 LET F$(Z)=F$(B)
500 LET F$(B)=Q$
510 GO TO 470
520 LET G=J: LET B=0
530 LET Z=1
540 LET B=Z+1
550 IF B>G THEN LET G=G-1: IF G
>0 THEN GO TO 530
560 IF G=0 THEN CLS : GO TO 20
570 IF E$(B)<E$(Z) THEN GO TO 5
90
580 LET Z=Z+1: GO TO 540
590 LET Q$=E$(Z)
600 LET E$(Z)=E$(B)
610 LET E$(B)=Q$
620 GO TO 580
630 FOR M=1 TO J
640 LPRINT F$(M)
650 NEXT M
660 RETURN
670 FOR M=1 TO J
680 LPRINT E$(M)
690 NEXT M
700 RETURN
710 PRINT "Enter name of artist
"
720 INPUT N$: LET N$=N$+"    "
```

```
 730 FOR M=1 TO J
 740 IF F$(M)( TO 4)=N$( TO 4) T
HEN GO TO 770
 750 NEXT M
 760 PRINT "Artist not found": P
AUSE 200: RETURN
 770 PRINT F$(M)
 780 PAUSE 0
 790 RETURN
 800 PRINT "Enter title"
 810 INPUT N$: LET N$=N$+"    "
 820 FOR M=1 TO J
 830 IF E$(M)( TO 4)=N$( TO 4) T
HEN GO TO 860
 840 NEXT M
 850 PRINT "Title not found": PA
USE 200: RETURN
 860 PRINT E$(M)
 870 PAUSE 0
 880 RETURN
```

SAMPLE OUTPUT FROM DATABASE

```
BEATLES:HELP:008
CHOPIN:WALTZ:34/3
MOZART:FANTASIA:K367
STONES:RAINBOW:DE3
VIVALDI:FOUR SEASONS:E3


FANTASIA:MOZART:K367
FOUR SEASONS:VIVALDI:E3
HELP:BEATLES:008
RAINBOW:STONES:DE3
WALTZ:CHOPIN:34/3
```

FINANCIAL MODEL/SALES PROJECTION

As I explained at the start of these programs, the FINANCIAL MODEL provides a crude version of a few of the facilities provided by spread sheet calculator programs like Visicalc. This program is designed to take monthly sales figures, or number of rejects, or turnover in staff or any other count of an event which occurs fairly regularly and has been recorded at regular intervals, and from this information extrapolate future monthly returns, assuming all other factors remain the same.

When you run it, you'll first be asked if you want a "hard copy" (i.e. dumped to the printer) of the program's output. If you enter 1 for yes, all the important output of this program (which will not include all the user prompts) will be LPRINTed, as well as being displayed on the screen. Next you'll be asked: "For how many months are figures available?" Change months to days, or years or whatever time period you are working to. You will then be asked to enter the figure for each month. As it is set up at the moment, the program can cope with the input of 19 months. Change the "A – 1" at the start of line 100 to a zero if you have more than 19 months' data.

The Timex Sinclair will then work out the approximate change from month to month. Comparing month two with month one, month three with month two and so on. The average percentage change will then be given.

You are then able to make an extrapolation of results, specifying the number of months for which you want figures projected, and whether you want this projection based on the last month for which you have a figure or on the average result per month.

Once this has been provided, the menu allows you a number of choices:

1. Run the projection again (which means you can change the starting figure from average to last month, or vice versa, and over a longer or shorter period of time).
2. Run through output again, but without entering figures again (although you'll still have to answer prompts for the projection).
3. Run the program from the beginning (this wipes all current data).
4. Save this run on tape (which you'll then recapture by choosing option 2 of this menu after reloading).
5. Stop.

If you've run through the program once without the printer working, and you decide you'd like a hard copy, use 5 to stop the program when you reach the menu, then restart the program with GO TO 10 rather than RUN. Next, select item 2 from the menu, and you'll get your figures on to the printer without having to re-enter them.

FINANCIAL MODEL/SALES PROJECTON

```
10 REM FINANCIAL MODEL
      SALES PROJECTION
15 GO SUB 490
20 PRINT ''"For how many month
s are          figures available?
"
30 INPUT M: LET TOT=0
40 IF M<2 THEN GO TO 30
50 CLS : DIM A(M): DIM B(M)
60 POKE 23692,0
70 FOR A=1 TO M
80 PRINT AT 20,0;"Enter figure
for month "; FLASH 1; INK 2;A
90 INPUT A(A)
100 PRINT AT A-1,0; BRIGHT 1; P
APER 1; INK 7;" Month ";A;" ";T
AB (17-LEN STR$ A(A));A(A);"
"
105 IF Z=1 THEN LPRINT        " Mo
nth ";A;" ";TAB (17-LEN STR$ A(A
));A(A);"
"
```

```
110 LET TOT=TOT+A(A): NEXT A
115 PRINT AT 20,0;"
                     ";AT A,0;
120 LET AV=TOT/M: FOR B=2 TO M
130 LET B(B)=(100-(A(B-1)*100/A
(B)))
140 NEXT B
145 PAUSE 100
150 PRINT ''' FLASH 1; INK 1;"
Difference between months: "
155 IF Z=1 THEN LPRINT " Differ
ence between months: "
160 FOR A=2 TO M
170 PRINT "Month "; INK 1;A-1;
INK 0;TAB 5;"to month "; INK 1;A
; INK 0;" - ";INT (B(A)+.5);"%"
175 IF Z=1 THEN LPRINT "Month "
;A-1,"to month ";A;" - ";INT (B(
A)+.5);"%"
180 NEXT A
185 PAUSE 100
190 LET TOTAL=0
200 FOR A=2 TO M
210 LET TOTAL=TOTAL+B(A)
220 NEXT A
230 LET AVERAGE=INT (TOTAL*100/
(M-1))/100
235 PRINT ' INK 2;"-----------
----------------------"
236 IF Z=1 THEN LPRINT "-------
----------------------------"
240 PRINT '"Average change is "
; INK 1; FLASH 1;AVERAGE; INK 0;
FLASH 0;"%"
245 IF Z=1 THEN LPRINT "Average
change is ";AVERAGE;"%"
250 PAUSE 100
255 PRINT ' INK 2;"-----------
----------------------"
256 IF Z=1 THEN LPRINT "-------
----------------------------"
260 PRINT '"Now a projection of
change:"
265 IF Z=1 THEN LPRINT "Now a p
rojection of change:"
270 INPUT "How many month's pro
jection     do you want? ";NUMBE
R
280 PRINT '"Final recorded mont
h was ";A(M)
290 PRINT '"Average per month w
as ";10*(INT AV/10)
300 INPUT "Do you wish to base
projection   on 1 - Final month;
or              2 - Average month
?";D
305 PRINT ' INK 2;"-----------
----------------------"
306 IF Z=1 THEN LPRINT "-------
----------------------------"
310 LET E=(A(M) AND D=1)+((10*(
INT AV/10)) AND D=2)
315 PRINT '"Month 1,  recorded:
";A(M)
316 IF Z=1 THEN LPRINT "Month 1
,  recorded: ";A(M)
```

```
320 FOR A=2 TO NUMBER
325 POKE 23692,0
330 LET E=E+AVERAGE*E/100
340 PRINT "Month ";A;", project
ed: ";INT (E)
342 IF Z=1 THEN LPRINT "Month "
;A;", projected: ";INT (E)
345 NEXT A
350 PAUSE 100: POKE 23692,0
355 PRINT ' INK 2;"-------------
-----------------"
356 IF Z=1 THEN LPRINT "--------
-----------------"
360 PRINT ' INK 2; INVERSE 1;"E
nter your choice:"
370 PRINT 'TAB 3;"1 - To run pr
ojection again"
380 PRINT TAB 3;"2 - To run thr
ough output            again, but
 without               entering f
igures                 again"
390 PRINT TAB 3;"3 - To run the
 program              from the b
eginning"
400 PRINT TAB 3;"4 - To save th
is run          on tape"
405 PRINT TAB 3;"5 - To stop"
410 LET A$=INKEY$
420 IF A$="" THEN GO TO 410
430 IF A$="1" THEN GO TO 260
440 IF A$="2" THEN GO TO 150
450 IF A$="3" THEN RUN
460 IF A$="4" THEN SAVE "SALES"
470 IF A$="5" THEN STOP
480 GO TO 360
490 INPUT "Do you want hard cop
y of          output?
              1 - Yes
              2 - No";Z
500 IF Z<1 OR Z>2 THEN GO TO 49
0
510 RETURN
```

PART OF ONE OUTPUT: FINANCIAL MODEL

```
Month 1      1345
Month 2      1456
Month 3      1567
Month 4      1678
Month 5      1789
Difference between months:
Month 1            to month 2 - 8%
Month 2            to month 3 - 7%
Month 3            to month 4 - 7%
Month 4            to month 5 - 6%
------------------------------------
Average change is 6.88%
------------------------------------
Now a projection of change:
------------------------------------
Month 1, recorded: 1789
Month 2, projected: 1912
```

```
Month 3, projected: 2043
Month 4, projected: 2184
Month 5, projected: 2334
Month 6, projected: 2495
----------------------------

1 - To run projection again
2 - To run through output
    again, but without
    entering figures
    again
3 - To run the program
    from the beginning
4 - To save this run
    on tape
5 - To stop
```

Suggestions for Further Reading

Gilder, Jules H. *BASIC Computer Programs in Science and Engineering.* Rochelle Park, N.J.: Hayden Book Company, Inc., 1981.

Poole, Lou and Borchers, Mary. *Some Common BASIC Programs.* New York: McGraw-Hill, 1981.

Sternberg, Charles D. *BASIC Computer Programs for Business.* Rochelle Park, N.J.: Hayden Book Company, Inc., 1981.

Struble, George. *Business Information Processing with BASIC.* Reading, Mass.: Addison-Wesley Publishing Company, 1980.

5

Using the Timex Sinclair in Education

This chapter is written for those who wish to use the Timex Sinclair as an aid in teaching others, such as parents helping their children, or a teacher using the computer in class. However, there is no reason why you cannot use the programs and ideas, if you wish, to help yourself with revision for exams, or just for a little brain-stretching exercise. It is quite interesting how much you can learn just by trying to write a program which will help others learn. At the very least, you may well pick up a smattering of French, physics or whatever while looking up information to store in a quiz program's DATA statements.

Commercial, educational software for the Timex Sinclair (or any other computer for that matter) tends to suffer from one of two faults. It is either so simple and general that it is of little use to anyone, or is so specialized that it is of use to only a very few. Creating your own learning tools with the computer overcomes both these faults. You can tailor the program exactly to your needs: teaching and testing just those parts of courses which appear to need particular attention. The routines and programs discussed in this chapter can easily be adapted for your specific needs.

The chapter will concentrate on programs which give practice at basic skills—such as basic mathematics and (in the case of one program) knowledge of French. There are many other types of educational programs you could write which could teach new material, or perhaps take the place of time-consuming laboratory work (such as a program which "combines chemicals" in specified quantities, and showed the resultant mixtures). In most cases, you'll find that one or more of the programs given here will give you a starting point to produce the program you need.

Educational programs—as you'll see a little later on—do not have to be dull. Some teaching programs can even be written quite explicitly as games. Educational games require the players to develop and apply their knowledge in order to compete with other students. To work well, success should go to those who use their knowledge most effectively, and although random factors may play some part, they should not determine the outcome of the game.

Programs that teach new material can be very lengthy, as the programmer needs to anticipate all of the likely mistakes and misconceptions that may arise, and to provide correction sequences for them. The same material will need to be presented in a number of different ways so that a child who does not understand the first explanation may succeed when the information is presented in a different way.

This sounds extremely demanding, almost impossible, and a good "half-way house" to this sort of program is one which is written with the knowledge that the student has a particular text book with him or her as the program proceeds. Then the program can be used more as an intelligent guide to the book, than as a stand alone teacher. The program could, for example, say: "Now that you've shown that you understand that Lamaism's beliefs and worship derive from the Mahayana form of Buddhism, I'd like you to turn to page 26 of the textbook, and read how it was introduced into Tibet. When you've done that, come back to the computer and I'll ask you some questions about it." On return, the questions could check the material on page 26, and—if some lack of understanding was shown—direct the student to a specific position on that page, or to another reference to the topic somewhere else in the book. Using a program in this way ensures that a programmer's time is not tied up creating endless PRINT statements to cover every possibility, and means your Timex Sinclair can be used to help teach subjects which might otherwise seem far too complex to allow for a computer approach.

Projects are a regular feature of elementary school work, but students often have problems locating suitable information. The Sinclair can be used to store the information itself or it can be used to help with the location of a suitable source of information. Apart from the immediate benefits of this to students, it may well help them become aware of the increasing importance of information technology in modern society.

Simulations of other types allow you to carry out investigations which cannot be performed in real life. The Sinclair can use a mathematical model to predict the outcome of making changes to a system. You might wish, for example, to find out how pollution levels will affect fish, insect and plant life in a pond. A simulation in economics will allow you to alter the money supply, and see how this affects employment levels. A chemistry simulation might allow you to change the catalyst, temperature and pressure to optimize the yield of, say, sulphur dioxide in a sulphuric acid manufacturing plant. Of course, a simulation can only be totally realistic when the mathematical model is an accurate representation of the system. Even when it is not totally accurate, so long as students are informed of simplifications in the simulation, it can be still most instructive.

At the end of this chapter, I'll discuss some specific approaches to educational software which have proved successful for others, along with an idea of the kind of things which can easily be transformed into educational programs. However, first I'd like to discuss specific programs (some written by Jeff Warren, and others by myself) which will show different approaches to the production of educational software. Even if these programs are not of immediate use to you in this form, they should give you models to work from to produce your own programs.

Many educational programs use the RND function to set sums or to select questions at random, so that the learner does not become bored by a predictable sequence of questions. Our first program randomly generates simple division problems, but it can easily be altered to give practice in any basic mathematical skill.

Line 5 makes the user-defined graphics symbol D into an ordinary division sign as used in school work. Next the initial score, s, is made equal to zero. The program sets 20 questions using a FOR/NEXT loop with q as the question number (lines 20–120). The questions take the form "What is 32 divided by 4?", which the Timex Sinclair sets up as x/y. Line 30 gives a value of y between 2 and 12, and line 40 produces a value of x which will give a whole number between 1 and 12 as the final answer. Line 50 displays the question and accepts the answer using INPUT a. Line 60 chooses between the correction sequence of lines 70 and 80, or the praise given by line 90, which also updates the score. Remember, you have to press both the CAPS SHIFT and the 9 key at the same time to obtain the graphics cursor, G, before typing the D in line 80. The D will change into ÷ when you run the program.

Line 100 enables the user to continue to the next problem when he or she is ready for it. How quickly a student can take in the information on the screen varies considerably, so that a fixed delay is not a good idea. PAUSE could be used instead, but you would have to set a long enough time or the message might disappear before it had been read, and once gone, the student could never get it back. Never force the user to wait for the next part of the program by using FOR/NEXT loops to create inflexible delays, as this can be very frustrating. Note that line 100 allows you to stop the program prematurely by keying in "s" before pressing ENTER. The last line of the program prints the final score.

DIVISION TEST

```
   5 FOR f=0 TO 7: READ a: POKE
USR "d"+f,a: NEXT f: DATA 0,16,0
,254,0,16,0,0
  10 LET s=0
  20 FOR q=1 TO 20
  30 LET y=2+INT (RND*11)
```

```
 40 LET x=y*INT (RND*12+1)
 50 PRINT AT 9,0; PAPER 6; "Ques
tion ";q''; PRINT "What is ";x;"
 divided by ";y;"?": INPUT a
 60 IF a=x/y THEN GO TO 90
 70 PRINT PAPER 6; ''"Wrong. The
answer is not ";a
 80 PRINT ''x;" D ";y;" = ";x/y
: PRINT PAPER 6; '"(remember that
";y;" x ";x/y;" = ";x;" )": GO
TO 100
 90 PRINT ''"Good, ";a;" is cor
rect.": LET s=s+1
 100 INPUT "Press ENTER to conti
nue.";c$: IF c$="s" THEN STOP
 110 CLS
 120 NEXT q
 130 PRINT AT 0,4;"You scored ";
s;" out of 20"
```

Make sure that you limit the difficulty of your questions to the capabilities of the student. Do not allow the computer to produce questions like
"What is 19 divided by 7?" if the student knows nothing of remainders and
decimals.

You can make your program more responsive to the user by using the
score to control the difficulty of the questions. One way of achieving this in
the division program is to rewrite line 30 as:

```
30  LET y=2+INT(RND*(3 + (s>=5)*4 + (s>=10)*4))
```

Until the score of correct answers reaches five, y will be set in the range 2 to
4, because the logical expressions $(s>=5)$ and $(s>=10)$ will both equal
zero, as both expressions are false. When the score is five or more, the
expression $(s>=5)$ becomes true and takes the value 1, and y will be given
a value between 2 and 8. Finally, when the score reaches ten, y will be
given a maximum value of 12. Similarly you can change line 40 to:

```
40  LET X = y* INT(RND*(5 + (s>=5)*7) + 1)
```

The advantage of this type of program control is that the transition to
harder problems is smooth, and the exercise will be both easier and more
pleasant for the user.

Although the program has been written for division problems, it is an
easy matter to change it to other types of calculation. We can change the
second part of line 50 to:

```
"What is 1/";y;" of ";x;"?"
```

This now gives questions of the type "What is ¼ of 32?" for practice
with fractions. You will need to change line 80 to match the new question
format. Try writing versions of the program to cover addition, subtraction
(remember to make the first number larger than the second, unless the
student knows about negative numbers) and multiplication.

Many programmers like to make their software more personal by having the computer respond to the user by name. The idea is that it makes the machine appear more human. If you wish to do this, you will need to write a subroutine which can converse in the following manner:

> *Timex Sinclair: "Hello. What is your name?"*
>
> *Student: "Samantha"*
>
> *Timex Sinclair: "Well Samantha, I hope that you are ready to answer some questions about the anatomy of the rat."*

This can be carried further by having a list of "praise phrases," one of which is selected at random for each correct answer:

> *"That's right Samantha, tibia was correct."*

or

> *"Well done Samantha, femur was correct."*

This type of approach gives a lot of satisfaction to some children, especially those who enjoy the talking computers and robots of science fiction.

The Timex Sinclair can also use children's competitive instincts by maintaining a best score record, together with a fastest time, if you make use of the system variable FRAMES to time how long it takes to answer a question. This works well if you have a student trying to better his or her own previous performance, but can be discouraging for the slower children in a group, so you should give careful thought to its use.

The next program, ARITHMETIC QUIZ, shows the student's name being used by the computer, and—in general—has a far more friendly approach than that used in the DIVISION program. As well, it allows the student to choose which type of question (addition, subtraction, multiplication or division) will be generated.

ARITHMETIC QUIZ

```
10 REM ARITHMETIC QUIZ
30 PRINT ''"Hello, there."''"
We're going to try a few sums."
40 PAUSE 200
50 CLS
60 PRINT '''"Now, what is your
name?"
70 INPUT A$
80 CLS
90 PRINT '''"Pleased to meet y
ou, "; FLASH 1; BRIGHT 1; INK 1;
A$
100 PRINT '''"Press any key whe
n you're ready";TAB 6;"to start.
"
```

```
110 PAUSE 0: LET SCORE=0
120 CLS
130 PRINT '"Now, ";A$;", I can
give you"'"questions on:"
140 PRINT '"1 - addition;"
150 PRINT '"2 - subtraction;"
160 PRINT '"3 - multiplication;
or"
170 PRINT '"4 - division."
180 PRINT ''"Enter a number fro
m "; FLASH 1;"1 to 4"'' FLASH 0;"
to tell me which type of sums"''
you want to try."
190 INPUT B$: LET B=VAL B$
200 IF B<1 OR B>4 THEN GO TO 19
0
205 CLS
210 PRINT '" OK, ";A$;", we'll
try some"'"sums using ";
220 PRINT INK 2; FLASH 1;("addi
tion" AND B=1)+("subtraction" AN
D B=2)+("multiplication" AND B=3
)+("division" AND B=4)
230 PAUSE 300
240 CLS
250 PRINT ''"Enter 1 if you wa
nt easy sums"'"or 5 if you want
fairly"'"difficult ones."'''"(Yo
u can enter 2, 3 or 4 if you"'"w
ant questions which are not"'"to
o easy, and not too hard.)"
260 INPUT C$: LET C=VAL C$
270 IF C<1 OR C>5 THEN GO TO 26
0
275 CLS
280 LET D$=("+" AND B=1)+("-" A
ND B=2)+("*" AND B=3)+("/" AND B
=4)
290 FOR E=1 TO 10
300 LET A=INT (RND*(10+C))+C
310 LET B=INT (RND*(10+4*C))+C
320 LET G$=STR$ A+D$+STR$ B
325 IF ABS (INT VAL G$)<>VAL G$
THEN GO TO 300
330 PRINT "Now, ";A$;", this is
";TAB 8;"question number ";E
340 PRINT ''"What is ";G$;"?"
350 PAUSE 50
360 PRINT ''"Try it now, and t
ype in"'"your answer"
370 INPUT F
372 LET NOTE=F+SCORE
375 IF NOTE>25 THEN LET NOTE=NO
TE/2: GO TO 375
380 IF F=VAL G$ THEN BEEP .08,N
OTE: BEEP 1,2*NOTE: PRINT FLASH
1; INK RND*7; PAPER 9;"Well done
, ";A$: LET SCORE=SCORE+1
390 IF F<>VAL G$ THEN PRINT "No
, I'm sorry, ";A$;", but"'"the a
nswer is ";VAL G$
400 PAUSE 50
410 PRINT ''"Your score is now
"; INK 1; FLASH 1;SCORE; INK 0;
FLASH 0;" out of ";E
```

```
 420 IF E<10 THEN PRINT ''''"Pres
s any key for the next question.
": PAUSE 0: CLS : NEXT E
 430 PAUSE 100
 440 CLS
 450 PRINT ''"That brings us to
the end of"'"that quiz, ";A$;"."
 460 PAUSE 100
 465 PRINT '''"Your score was ";
INK 1; FLASH 1;SCORE; INK 0; FL
ASH 0;" out of ";E;TAB 8; FLASH
1; BRIGHT 1; INK 2;SCORE*100/E;"
%"
 470 PRINT ''"Would you like ano
ther round?"'"Type in "Y" if you
would, or"'"press any key to en
d."
 480 INPUT Y$
 490 IF Y$="Y" OR Y$="y" THEN GO
TO 100
 500 PRINT '''"It's been good do
ing sums with"'"you, ";A$
 520 PRINT ''' FLASH 1;"See you
again sometime"
 530 STOP
```

As you'll see when you run it, color and FLASH have been used to highlight certain things (such as the student's name the first time it is used). The conversation of this program proceeds as follows:

> *"Hello, there.*
> *"We're going to try a few sums.*
> *"Now, what is your name?"* (Student enters his or her name)
> *"Pleased to meet you (FLASH, BRIGHT, blue INK), Samantha.*
> *"Press any key when you're ready to start."*

PAUSE 0 is used here (line 110) to hold the display until a key is pressed. The variable SCORE (which holds the score, naturally enough) is set to zero, and the screen clears (line 120). The computer takes up the conversation again:

> *"Now, Samantha, I can give you questions on:*
> *1—addition;*
> *2—subtraction;*
> *3—multiplication; or*
> *4—division."*

> *"Enter a number from (FLASH on) 1 to 4 (FLASH off) to tell me which type of sums you want to try."*

The student enters a number which, as you can see from line 190, is accepted as a string and then converted (using VAL) to a number.

By the way, it is important to write programs so that incorrect input doesn't cause a crash. This is not fully covered in the first program in this chapter, the division program, in which the input of a letter instead of a number could cause the program to stop with an error message, leaving the user wondering what to do. This problem can be overcome by treating every input as a string variable.

You can use the CODE function to make sure that the input is numeric, if that is what you require. Then you can convert the string into a number using VAL. Try the following lines for a single-digit number.

```
10   INPUT n$
20   IF LEN n$<>1 THEN PRINT "Single digit please,
     GO TO 10
30   IF CODE n$<48 OR CODE n$>57 THEN PRINT
     "Numbers only please," : GO TO 10
40   LET n = VAL n$: PRINT "At last,"
```

Run it to see that you can only complete the program by entering a single-digit number. Numbers have character codes from 48 to 57 inclusive.

For multi-digit numbers you will have to separate the input into individual characters using string slicing techniques and check each character in turn. As an alternative you could use INKEY$ = to get the number one digit at a time, with CODE INKEY$ = 13 (which is the character code for ENTER) terminating the input.

Now, back to our ARITHMETIC QUIZ. The computer has asked the user to enter a number from one to four to select the type of questions which will be asked. The conversation continues:

> "OK, Samantha, we'll try some sums using subtraction (or whatever Samantha had chosen)".

Note how line 220 uses Timex Sinclair's way of evaluating the logical expression AND to choose one of the four words (addition, subtraction, multiplication or division) depending on the value which has been given to B. There is a PAUSE (line 230) and the screen clears. The talkative Timex Sinclair continues: "Enter 1 if you want easy sums, or 5 if you want fairly difficult ones. (You can enter 2, 3, or 4 if you want questions which are not too easy, and not too hard.)" This gives the user a measure of control over the program, and the interactive nature of the experience to this point should help the user feel he or she really is conversing with a "robot intelligence" with a personality. The input is accepted as a string and converted to a number, and again the screen clears. Line 280 makes use of the AND logic evaluation again to determine the arithmetic sign $(+, -, *$ or $/)$ which will be used in presenting questions to the user.

Line 290 starts the loop of 10 questions which will be presented to the student, with lines 300 and 310 choosing numbers for the problem, with the size of the number being related to the degree of difficulty (variable C) requested by the student back in line 260. Line 320 adds the numbers and the arithmetic sign chosen together into a single string. Line 325 checks the result of this problem, to ensure that the answer is not fractional (as it might be if the sum was a division), nor negative (as it could be in a subtraction problem). This validation line can be left out if answers which are not whole numbers, nor above zero, are acceptable.

Line 330 prints out the question, using the student's name again:

> *"Now, Samantha, this is question number 4*
> *"What is 7 + 3?"* (There is a slight PAUSE, line 350)
> *"Try it now, and type in your answer."*

Line 380 checks the answer, and, if it is correct, rewards the student with a couple of beeps, whose pitch is related to the number of correct answers which have been obtained so far in the current test. The words "Well done, Samantha" are printed on the screen, in a randomly selected flashing color (using INK 9 to ensure that the words can be read), and the SCORE is incremented by one. If the answer given is wrong, line 390 prints up "No, I'm sorry, Samantha, but the answer is 10". Notice that there are no flashing words, nor beeps for a wrong answer, so the correct answer includes a better reward than an incorrect one.

There is another short PAUSE, and the Timex Sinclair prints up: "Your score is now (INK 1, FLASH) 1 (FLASH off, INK normal) out of 3". If the tenth question has not been asked, the computer then says: "Press any key for the next question." This waiting for a key press allows a student to proceed at the pace he or she feels most comfortable with.

At the end of the tenth question, after a PAUSE, the screen clears:

> *"That brings us to the end of that quiz, Samantha."*
> (PAUSE)
> *"Your score was* (INK 1, FLASH) *8* (INK normal, FLASH
> off) *out of 10.* (many effects) *80%*
> *"Would you like another round? Type in "Y" if you would,*
> *or press any key to end."*

Although it can take quite a long time to write a conversational program like this, the increased interaction it creates with the student more than repays the time spent in creating the extra lines in the program.

Line 480 accepts the student's answer, and line 490 checks if it is a "Y" or a "y", thus sidestepping the problem of determining whether the computer has CAPS LOCK engaged or not.

If the student says another test is required, the computer does not just RUN from the beginning, as this would wipe the student's name from the computer memory, and the whole "Now, what is your name?" sequence would have to be repeated, which would convincingly destroy the illusion of an intelligent, helpful robot. Instead, the computer goes to the point in the program (line 100) which follows the "What is your name?" routine. If the student has not answered "Y" or "y" to the question regarding a further test, the computer prints up: "It's been good doing sums with you, Samantha. *(FLASH on)* See you again sometime."

Although this explanation has been even longer than the program, I hope it shows just how effective even a simple program can be made with the use of 'conversation'. Comparing the output of ARITHMETIC QUIZ with the DIVISION program shows how much more user friendly the second program is than the first.

There are other ways to make programs user friendly, by giving more feedback than just "Well done" messages. Many children welcome the additional motivation provided by linking the "school" exercise to some form of game or visually interesting reward. We are now going to extend the first program in this chapter in this way, making use of Timex Sinclair's user-defined color graphics and the sound generator.

At the top of the screen the program will show a river with an incomplete bridge, and a tank on the left bank. Each time a sum is correctly answered, the deck of the bridge is extended. If all twenty answers are correct, a success tune is played, the tank crosses the completed bridge and fires its gun.

First replace line 5 of the DIVISION program by:

```
5   GO TO 150
```

and add to the end of line 90:

```
:GO SUB 250
```

Change line 110 to read:

```
110 PRINT AT 8,0; FOR n=1 to 11:PRINT b$: NEXT n
```

Now add the following lines to your program.

ADDITIONAL LINES FOR DIVISION:

```
140>IF s=20 THEN PAUSE 75: GO T
O 260
145 STOP
150 FOR n=1 TO 4:  READ s$
160 FOR m=0 TO 7:  READ a:  POKE
USR s$+m,a:  NEXT m
170 NEXT n
180 DATA "a",7,15,7,255,255,127
,63,27
190 DATA "b",192,254,192,255,25
5,255,254,108
```

```
200 DATA "c",255,0,0,0,0,0,0,0
 210 DATA "d",0,16,0,254,0,16,0,
0
 220 LET b$="  "
 230 PRINT AT 3,0;"AB": PRINT P
APER 4;"      ": PRINT AT 4,5;"
         ": PRINT AT 4,24
; PAPER 4;"        ": PRINT PAPE
R 1;b$;b$
 240 GO TO 10
 250 PRINT AT 4,3+s; OVER 1;"C":
RETURN
 260 FOR n=0 TO 10: FOR m=4 TO 8
STEP .5: BEEP 0.01,m+n: NEXT m:
NEXT n
 270 FOR n=0 TO 23: PRINT AT 3,n
;" AB": PAUSE 5: NEXT n
 280 FOR n=1 TO 50: PLOT 216,150
: DRAW INK 2;36,0: PLOT 216,150:
DRAW INK 7;36,0: NEXT n
 290 PRINT AT 9,10;"well done."
```

Lines 150 to 170 set up four user-defined graphics symbols, using the data held in lines 180 to 210. The b$ defined by line 210 is used in line 110 to clear part of the screen only, leaving the picture of the bridge and tank undisturbed. This picture is created by line 230. You will have to obtain the graphics cursor before typing "AB", as this will be the tank. The same applies to the "C" in line 250 and to the "AB" in line 270.

Line 250 draws a new section of the bridge roadway after each correct answer. Line 260 plays the victory tune if all of the answers are correct, line 270 drives the tank over the bridge and line 280 fires its gun.

Here's what it looks like in action:

Question 2

What is 10 divided by 5?

Good, 2 is correct.

Press ENTER to continue.

```
Question 12
What is 18 divided by 9?

Wrong. The answer is not 3

18 ÷ 9 = 2
(remember that 9 x 2 = 18 )

Press ENTER to continue.
```

```
You scored 20 out of 20
```

```
well done.
```

You can, of course, link the tank sequence to any educational program to provide additional motivation. However, if you use it too often, it may lose its appeal. Try making up sequences of your own, bearing the following points in mind. Ensure that the reward section does not interfere with the educational aspects of the program. If it takes longer than a second or so after each question, it will soon become tedious and annoying. The incentive should be positive, encouraging the child to pursue success rather than to avoid disaster. Do not penalize failure, because this makes some children feel anxious, which does not make for enjoyable learning.

You can be fairly flexible in your approach to writing educational programs. There is no particular reason, for example, why the computer should *always* be used to both generate problems, and check their answers. Our next program, EQUATIONS (which generates equations of the type $ax + by = z$), for example, only works out a problem and prints it on the screen. When the student wants to see the answer, he or she simply presses any key (except BREAK) and the answer, along with the values substituted in the original equations, is given. You may well wish to enter this program into your Timex Sinclair and, as an exercise, add a full conversational framework, a score-keeping mechanism, and a means of accepting and evaluating the student's answers.

EQUATIONS

```
 10 REM EQUATIONS
 20 INK 7: PAPER 1
 30 BORDER 1: CLS
 40 DEF FN M(N)=INT (RND*N)+1
 50 LET A=FN M(10)
 60 LET B=FN M(10)
 70 LET C=FN M(10)
 80 LET D=FN M(10)
 90 LET X=FN M(10)
100 LET Y=FN M(10)
110 LET E=A*X+B*Y
120 LET F=C*X+D*Y
130 PRINT ''' INK 6;"The equati
ons are:"
140 PRINT 'TAB 8; INVERSE 1;A;'
x + ";B;"y = ";E
150 PRINT 'TAB 8; INVERSE 1;C;'
x + ";D;"y = ";F
160 PRINT ''"You must solve them
 for "; INVERSE 1;"x"; INVERSE 0
;" and "; INVERSE 1;"y"
170 PRINT '''"Press any key for
the solution"
180 PAUSE 0
190 CLS
200 PRINT ''''TAB 8;A;"x + ";B;
"y = ";E
210 PRINT 'TAB 8;C;"x + ";D;"y
= ";F
220 PRINT 'TAB 4;"The value of
x is "; FLASH 1;X
230 PRINT 'TAB 4;"The value of
y is "; FLASH 1;Y
240 PRINT 'TAB 8,A;"*";X;" + ";
B;"*";Y;" = ";E
250 PRINT 'TAB 8;C;"*";X;" + ";
D;"*";Y;" = ";F
260 PRINT '''"Press any key for
 a new problem"
270 PAUSE 0
280 RUN
```

SAMPLE RUN: EQUATIONS

```
The equations are:
        3x + 1y = 13
        7x + 1y = 25
You must solve them for x and y

Press any key for the solution
        3x + 1y = 13
        7x + 1y = 25
    The value of x is 3
    The value of y is 4
        3*3 + 1*4 = 13
        7*3 + 1*4 = 25


Press any key for a new problem

The equations are:
        9x + 5y = 120
        9x + 6y = 126
You must solve them for x and y

Press any key for the solution
        9x + 5y = 120
        9x + 6y = 126
    The value of x is 10
    The value of y is 6
        9*10 + 5*6 = 120
        9*10 + 6*6 = 126


    Press any key for a new problem
```

Our next program, CATS AND THINGS, is for very young children. It uses INKEY$ throughout, and has rigorous input validation. A random number of tanks, trucks or cats are displayed on the screen, and the child has to type in the correct number.

Note the difference between the use of INPUT and INKEY$. INPUT does give you the chance to correct mistakes. INKEY$ has the advantage for single character inputs that you do not subsequently have to press ENTER. This makes the program quicker to use and gives it a more professional finish.

The tanks, trucks or cats are printed with the user-defined graphics symbols A and B, the necessary data being held in lines 510 to 530. The type of object is selected randomly in line 20, and the computed RESTORE sets the DATA pointer to the correct line. Lines 30 to 70 then assign the name of the object to n$, and set up the graphics symbols.

Lines 80 to 140 choose the number of objects, print them at the screen positions specified by the data in line 600, and ask the child how many objects there are. Note that you must have the G cursor when you type AB in line 120. BEEP is used in conjunction with the visual display to direct the child's attention in the correction section (lines 180 to 230). Praise, accompanied by a rising sequence of notes, is given by lines 250 and 260.

You may wish to improve this program by adding extra statements to keep the score and to print it at the end of a set of 10 questions. You could also make the display more attractive by introducing a random INK color into line 140. Avoid white cats on a white background, as children feel cheated when they forget to count them. Try increasing the range of objects—how about birds or spiders? Give your children some squared paper and get them to devise some of their own. Write additional DATA lines from 540, and increase the number in line 10 from 3 to your total number of different types of object. Another variation would be to have random positions for the objects, if you feel that the domino-type pattern encourages convergent thinking.

CATS AND THINGS

```
  5 LET b$="
                "
 10 LET i=1+INT (RND*3)
 15 REM CHOOSE AND FORM OBJECT
 20 RESTORE 500+10*i
 30 READ n$
 40 FOR n=1 TO 2: READ s$
 50 FOR m=0 TO 7
 60 READ a: POKE USR s$+m,a
 70 NEXT m: NEXT n
 75 REM PRINT RND NO OF OBJECT
 80 LET z=1+INT (RND*9)
 90 RESTORE 600
100 FOR n=1 TO z
110 READ x,y
120 PRINT AT x,y;"AB"
130 NEXT n
140 PRINT AT 15,0;"How many ";n
$;" are there?"
150 GO SUB 410
160 IF CODE i$<48 OR CODE i$>57
THEN GO TO 150
170 IF i$=STR$ z THEN GO TO 250
175 REM CORRECTION SEQUENCE
180 PRINT AT 15,0;b$: RESTORE 6
00
190 FOR n=1 TO z
```

```
200  READ x,y
210  PRINT AT x,y-1; PAPER 6;n
220  BEEP 1,n
230  NEXT n
240  GO TO 280
245  REM PRAISE
250  PRINT AT 15,0;"Good.";b$:  P
RINT AT 7,0; FLASH 1;z
260  FOR m=0 TO 4 STEP .1: BEEP
0.02,m*m: NEXT m: BEEP 1,20
270  PRINT AT 7,0;z
280  PRINT AT 21,0;"Press ENTER"
290  GO SUB 410
300  IF CODE i$<>13 THEN GO TO 2
90
310  CLS : GO TO 10
400  REM SINGLE KEY INPUT
410  IF INKEY$<>"" THEN GO TO 41
0
420  IF INKEY$="" THEN GO TO 420
430  LET i$=INKEY$
440  RETURN
500  REM DATA
510  DATA "tanks","a",7,15,7,255
,255,127,63,27,"b",192,254,192,2
55,255,255,254,108
520  DATA "cats","a",0,128,127,6
3,63,56,40,40,"b",28,28,252,240,
240,80,80,80
530  DATA "trucks","a",0,0,0,255
,255,255,255,48,"b",28,30,30,255
,255,255,255,12
600  DATA 4,5,10,5,4,11,10,11,7,
8,4,18,10,18,4,24,10,24
```

SAMPLE RUN: CATS AND THINGS

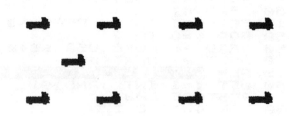

How many trucks are there?

How many cats are there?

So far in this chapter we've been concentrating on numerical problems, which are the easiest ones to write for the Timex Sinclair. But there is no reason to assume that ones requiring verbal answers need be much more difficult.

The next program, FRENCH VOCABULARY, stores the questions and answers in DATA statements, and can easily be extended or adapted for any similar one word answer quiz programs. Notice in this program that the computer must have CAPS LOCK engaged, as the questions, and the answers the computer is checking, are all in capital letters. The program allows the student to choose the number of questions he or she wishes to try (line 80) and this number is used in the FOR/NEXT loop in line 100.

You may believe it is important in programs of this type to ensure that the same question is not asked more than once in a run. If you do, you may wish to use or adapt the mechanism given in this program which ensures the meaning of the same word is not asked for more than once in any run. Line 30 dimensions an array and, as you know, sets every element of that array to zero. You can see in the DATA statements that the word in English is followed by the word in French, which is in turn followed by a number. When a pair of words is chosen (by randomly reading through the DATA statement, see lines 110 to 130), a value is also assigned to the variable X. Each pair of words has a unique number, and this element of the array is set to the value 1 in line 160. Line 150 checks to see if this element is 1 before printing up the question, and if it is, RESTOREs, and then goes to choose another pair of words (and flag number). Although this means it takes a little longer at the end of the quiz to find an unused pair of words than it does at the beginning, you'll find the delay adds to, rather than detracts from, the program when it is running.

You'll see that this program, like most of the earlier ones, responds to a correct answer with a greater flourish than it does to an answer which is wrong. Notice also that the program gives an immediate correction if the student is wrong.

FRENCH VOCABULARY

```
  10 REM FRENCH VOCABULARY
  20 LET SCORE=0: PAPER 1: INK 7
BORDER 1: CLS
  30 DIM A(20)
  40 PRINT ''TAB 6;"Welcome to t
his French"
  50 PRINT TAB 8;"vocabulary tes
t."
  60 PRINT ''TAB 6;"How many wor
ds would"
  70 PRINT "     you like to try?
(1 to 20)"
  80 INPUT B
  90 IF B<1 OR B>20 THEN GO TO 8
0
 100 FOR C=1 TO B
 110 FOR D=1 TO INT (RND*20)+1
 120 READ E$: READ F$: READ X
 130 NEXT D
 140 RESTORE : CLS
 150 IF A(X)=1 THEN GO TO 110
 160 LET A(X)=1
 170 PRINT '' INK RND*7; PAPER
9;" Question number ";C;": "
 180 PRINT '''"What is the Frenc
h for";TAB 4;E$;"?"
 190 INPUT A$
 200 IF A$=F$ THEN LET SCORE=SCO
RE+1: BEEP .1,2.5*SCORE: PRINT F
LASH 1; INK 2; PAPER 5;'''" Yes,
 ";F$;" is correct "
 210 IF A$<>F$ THEN PRINT ''"No,
 I'm sorry."''"The French word i
or ";E$;TAB 8;"is ";F$
 220 IF C<B THEN PRINT '' INK 3;
 FLASH 1; BRIGHT 1;" Your score
is now ";SCORE;" "
 230 PAUSE 150
 240 NEXT C
 250 INK 2: PAPER 7: FLASH 1: CL
S : PRINT AT 6,3;"In that test y
ou scored ";SCORE
 260 PAUSE 200: FLASH 0
 270 RUN
 280 DATA "EVERYWHERE","PARTOUT"
,1,"SELDOM","RAREMENT",2,"OFTEN"
,"SOUVENT",3,"NEVER","JAMAIS",4,
"ALWAYS","TOUJOURS",5
 290 DATA "VERY","TRES",6,"MORE"
,"PLUS",7,"LESS","MOINS",8,"YES"
,"OUI",9,"NO","NON",10
 300 DATA "THANK YOU","MERCI",11
,"ONE","UN",12,"TWO","DEUX",13,"
THREE","TROIS",14,"FOUR","QUATRE
",15
```

```
310 DATA "FIVE","CINQ",16,"SIX"
,"SIX",17,"SEVEN","SEPT",18,"EIG
HT","HUIT",19,"NINE","NEUF",20
320 STOP
```

SAMPLE RUN: FRENCH VOCABULARY

```
    Welcome to this French
        vocabulary tes..

    How many words would
you like to try? (1 to 20)



 Question number 1:

What is the French for
    MORE?
PLUS


 Yes, PLUS is correct

 Your score is now 1




 Question number 2:

What is the French for
    EVERYWHERE?
PARTUOT


No, I'm sorry.

The French word for EVERYWHERE
        is PARTOUT

 Your score is now 1




 Question number 3:

What is the French for
    FIVE?
CINQ


 Yes, CINQ is correct

 Your score is now 2
```

You can use the next program, QUIZ-MASTER, for anything from weekly spelling lists to advanced biology. The catch is that you have to provide the questions. This is easier than you might think, and ideally students will do most of the work for you.

The program is used to store a selection of questions or clues, together with the appropriate answers. Here are some examples to start you off:

What is the French for "to give?"
(*answer:* donner)

Name the mineral mined at St. Austell.
(*answer:* china-clay)

Which subatomic particle has 1 unit of mass and no charge?
(*answer:* neutron)

Which cell organelles contain the cytochromes?
(*answer:* mitochondria)

Short, simple clues should be sufficient for the weekly spelling test. If the list includes "knight," a suitable clue would be "armed horseman." Persuade your child to type in his or her own clues and words, and then try the test yourself to make sure that you agree on the spellings.

The program first flashes the complete set of answers briefly onto the screen one at a time. It then presents the questions in random order, but without any repeats. If you get one wrong, or simply press ENTER, you are given a hint, "k....t" for *knight*, or "d....r" for *donner*. RUN 500 allows you to create a new set of questions and answers.

QUIZ MASTER

```
  10 REM INITIALISATION
  20 LET s=0: LET x=m: LET b$="-
---------------": LET e$="
                            "
  30 FOR n=1 TO m: LET y(n)=n: N
EXT n
  40 GO SUB 400: CLS : FOR n=1 T
O m: PRINT AT 10,8;a$(n): PAUSE
50: CLS : NEXT n
  50 REM MAIN PROGRAM
  60 LET z=INT (RND*x+1): LET q=
y(z)
  70 LET x=x-1
  80 FOR n=z TO x: LET y(n)=y(n+
1): NEXT n
  90 CLS : LET t=2
 100 PRINT AT 3,0;c$(q): INPUT i
$
 110 IF i$<>a$(q) ( TO ((q)) THEN
 GO TO 240
 120 LET s=s+t: GO TO 210
 130 GO SUB 410: CLS
 140 IF x>0 THEN GO TO 60
```

```
150 REM FINAL SCORE
160 PRINT AT 5,0;"Your score wa
s ";s;" out of ";m*2
170 STOP
200 REM PRAISE
210 PRINT AT 7,0;"Well done, ";
i$;" was right.";AT 9,15;e$
220 GO TO 130
230 REM WRONG ANSWER
240 IF i$="" THEN GO TO 260
245 PRINT AT 7,0;i$;" was wrong
.";e$;AT 9,0;e$
250 GO SUB 410
260 IF t=2 THEN GO TO 310
270 PRINT AT 7,0;"The right ans
wer was:";e$;AT 9,15;a$(q)
280 GO TO 130
300 REM HINT SECOND TRY
310 LET t=1
320 PRINT AT 7,0;"Here is a hin
t:";e$;AT 21,0;e$
330 PRINT AT 9,15;a$(q,1)+b$(1
TO l(q)-2)+a$(q,l(q))
340 GO TO 100
400 REM ENTER TO CONTINUE
410 PRINT AT 21,0;"Press ENTER
to continue."
420 GO SUB 450
430 IF CODE k$=13 THEN RETURN
440 GO TO 420
450 REM SINGLE KEY INPUT
460 IF INKEY$<>"" THEN GO TO 46
0
470 IF INKEY$="" THEN GO TO 470
480 LET k$=INKEY$: RETURN
500 REM ENTER QUESTIONS AND ANS
WERS
510 PRINT "How many questions?"
: INPUT m
520 DIM c$(m,64): DIM a$(m,15):
DIM l(m): DIM y(m)
530 FOR q=1 TO m
540 CLS : PRINT "Question ";q''
550 PRINT "Type in the question
or clue.": INPUT c$(q)
560 PRINT 'c$(q)''"Type in the
answer.": INPUT i$
570 PRINT 'i$;AT 20,0;"If satis
factory, type s;","to delete typ
e d."
580 GO SUB 460
590 IF k$="d" THEN GO TO 540
600 IF k$<>"s" THEN GO TO 580
610 LET l(q)=LEN i$: LET a$(q)=
i$
620 NEXT q
650 REM SAVE AND RUN
660 CLS : INPUT "What is the pr
ogram name?";p$
670 SAVE p$ LINE 20
```

To understand how this program works it is best to start where the
questions and answers are fed in, from line 500 onwards. The total num-

ber of questions, m, obtained in line 510 is used to dimension four arrays in line 520. Array c$ holds m questions, each up to 64 characters (two lines) long. Array a$ holds the m answers, each up to 15 characters long. If you want longer questions or answers, then change these DIM statements. Array 1 is used to hold the real lengths of the answers, as the answer strings are padded out with spaces when they are stored in the array. The answer length is used when the child's answer is compared with the correct one.

The answers are initially accepted using INPUT i$, so that their lengths can be determined before they are stored in array a$.

Lines 660 and 670 force you to save your program immediately. As you have stored all of your questions and answers in arrays, they will be cleared from memory if you use RUN. If you wish to rerun the program you must use GO TO 20, as this leaves your questions and answers intact. You might like to write a few lines at the end of the main program to give the choice of running the program again or not.

Returning to the start of the program, lines 20 and 30 initialize variables; s is the score, and x is the number of questions which have still to be asked; b$ is used to provide the hyphens in the hints, and e$ is used to clear single lines on the screen.

Line 40 flashes all of the answers onto the screen. This is a helpful memory-jogger for short sets of questions, but you should delete it when the number of questions is large.

The array y (dimensioned in line 520) stores the question numbers in a way that prevents annoying repetitions when the program is run. Line 30 initializes the arrays so that $y(1) = 1$, $y(2) = 2$ and so on. If there were only four questions in the test, then line 60 will give z a value between 1 and 4. Suppose that $z = 2$; the question number q is made equal to $y(2)$, which is 2. Line 70 decreases x, the number of questions left. Line 80 eliminates question numbers which have been used.

Before line 80	After line 80
y(1)=1	y(1)=1
y(2)=2	y(2)=3
y(3)=3	y(3)=4
y(4)=4	y(4)=4

You get two points if you answer the question correctly at the first attempt, and one point at the second attempt. Line 110 uses the answer length l(q) in a string slicer to remove the spaces which pad out the answer word when it is stored in array a$. You have to remove these spaces because

"Constantinople" <> "Constantinople   "

The answer length is again used in line 330 to slice the correct number of hyphens from b$ to make up the hint "C————".

You can use this program to reinforce children's school work in many subjects. If you feed French vocabulary, chemistry definitions and questions from English literature into the Timex Sinclair on a regular basis, you will soon establish a substantial bank of revision material (and will probably learn quite a bit yourself). The preliminary flash through the answers and the hint option make the responses come easily to mind when the program is run again at intervals throughout the year. This will give your child the confidence in the basic meanings of words and terms, without which further progress cannot be made in any subject. To enhance the program, you could use a further array to store explanations or additional information which can be called up or by-passed by the user at will. Another possible development would be to check wrong answers against a list of related terms, and to have the Timex Sinclair give the correct meaning of the child's answer.

From that very general educational program, we move to a very different, quite specific one. This one tests reading speed, and retention. The computer chooses from sentences stored in DATA statements from line 160, and prints them on the screen. They are held on the screen for a time related to the length of the phrase (see line 60) and then the screen is cleared, and the student is asked to enter the phrase he or she has just read into the computer. The phrase entered by the student is compared (except for its first letter, so the first letter can be upper or lower case) with the phrase (minus its first letter) generated by the computer.

If the two are the same a "Well done" message appears on the screen, and in due course the screen clears and another phrase is chosen. If the student gets the phrase wrong, there is a short pause, and it is repeated. This occurs until the phrase is typed in correctly.

You should alter the 20 at the end of line 60 to keep the phrase on the screen for as long as you think necessary for the reading ability of the child. The phrases used should, of course, also be altered to suit the age and ability of the child. If you like you can take the place of the computer, and get the child to repeat the phrase to you, rather than type it in, if this seems a better way of strengthening your child's reading ability.

READING TEST

```
 10 INK 1: PAPER 7: BORDER 7: CLS
 20 PAUSE 50: RESTORE
 30 FOR J=1 TO INT (RND*11) +1
 40 BEEP 1/J,3*J: READ A$: NEXT J
 50 PRINT AT 10,0;A$
 60 PAUSE (LEN A$) *20
 70 CLS
 80 INPUT INK 2;"Now enter the phrase you","have just read",,B$
```

```
  90 PRINT INVERSE 1;" ";B$;" "
 100 PAUSE 50
 110 IF A$(2 TO )=B$(2 TO ) THEN
BEEP .3,LEN A$: PRINT ''  INK 3;
FLASH 1;"Well done, that was co
rrect": PAUSE 300: RUN
 120 PRINT ''"Sorry, that was no
t right"
 130 PRINT ''"Here it is again"
 140 PAUSE 200: CLS
 150 GO TO 50
 160 DATA "Watch the dog run"
 170 DATA "The cat has four legs
"
 180 DATA "The egg is brown"
 190 DATA "The sun is hot"
 200 DATA "The fox runs quickly"
 210 DATA "The duck swims slowly
"
 220 DATA "The camel has a hump"
 230 DATA "The bell is ringing"
 240 DATA "The fish is wet"
 250 DATA "The book is open"
 260 DATA "The bus is red"
```

Children enjoy using the next program, DOODLE-BUG, to produce sketches and doodles, but we will be creating maps and diagrams with it. You can draw straight lines horizontally, vertically or diagonally using the keys shown below:

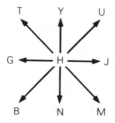

The "home" key H at the center has no effect.

DOODLE-BUG

```
 10 BORDER 6
 20 INPUT "Initial x coordinate
?";x
 30 INPUT "Initial y coordinate
?";y
 40 PLOT x,y
 70 LET c$=INKEY$
 80 LET x=x+(c$="u")+(c$="j")+(
c$="m")-(c$="t")-(c$="g")-(c$="b
")
 90 LET y=y+(c$="t")+(c$="y")+(
c$="u")-(c$="b")-(c$="n")-(c$="m
")
```

```
100 LET x=x-(x>255)+(x<0)
110 LET y=y-(y>175)+(y<0)
120 IF c$="s" THEN STOP
130 GO TO 40
```

Type in the program and run it. Select your starting position using the pixel x and y coordinates. Line 70 checks to see which key you are pressing, and sets c$ equal to this. Lines 80 and 90 change the x and y coordinates accordingly. If you press "m" then (c$ = "m") is true, and so take the value 1. The rest of the expressions in lines 80 and 90 are not true, and so equal 0. Thus $x = x + 1$, and $y = y + 1$, and the next point will be plotted one position to the southeast of the first. Lines 100 and 110 prevent you from going outside the plotting area, which would result in a crash. Line 120 allows you to stop sketching by pressing the "s" key.

You can save your works of art with SAVE "sketch" SCREEN$. This gives your picture the name "sketch", and stores it on tape. This simple sketchpad program can be embellished in a variety of ways. You can rewrite line 120 as:

```
120 IF c$ = "c" THEN GO TO 140
```

Entering "c" for change passes control to line 140. There you can write statements such as INPUT "Ink color?"; ink. Write INK ink; into line 40 after the PLOT statement, and you can now draw in color. You can include similar statements so that your repertoire includes PAPER, OVER, FLASH, BRIGHT and INVERSE. The results which you can obtain can be quite elaborate, as the following sample shows:

SAMPLE RUN DOODLE-BUG

What is the name of this town?

`Which of the numbered states is Queensland?`

The map of Australia was drawn using the original sketchpad program, modified by inserting the following two lines:

```
50  IF INKEY$ <>"" THEN GO TO 50
60  IF INKEY$ ="" THEN GO TO 60
```

This slows the program down so that it plots only one point each time you press a key. You need to find a map that is exactly the right size to fit the plotting area on your TV screen. Trace the map onto a sheet of transparent plastic, and tape this to your TV screen. Use the program to copy the map onto the screen. Leave some space on the screen for questions and answers.

When your outline is complete, save it. You can add to your map using direct commands; CIRCLE 55, 50, 2 will produce a small circle for a town. To find the coordinates of places on the map, use the program again. Draw a line to the required spot, stop the program, and print the values of *x* and *y* in a corner of the screen. Restart the program using GO TO 40 and repeat the process. Finally, reload a clean copy of the map, add your towns and cities, and save the finished version.

You can apply the same technique to produce almost anything you like, from circuit diagrams in physics to transverse sections of plant stems in biology.

The next task is to link your map or diagram to a question and answer program. If the QUIZ-MASTER program is used, it needs some modification. Replace line 40 with:

```
40  LOAD "map" SCREEN$
```

You will also have to direct all PRINT statements to the bottom of the screen. The following sub-routine may help:

```
350 REM CLEAR BOTTOM THREE LINES
360 PRINT AT 19,0;e$;e$;e$
```

```
370 PRINT AT 19,0;
380 RETURN
```

Now RUN 500 and enter your questions and answers. When you have saved this on tape, BREAK, and reload your map. Save this using SAVE "map" SCREEN$ onto the same tape immediately following the question and answer program. Now when you load QUIZ-MASTER, it will automatically load the map and go on to the questions.

As you've seen, in this chapter we've developed a range of programs which students will probably enjoy using, and which can be written without too large an investment of time. The programs fall mainly into the category of drill and practice exercises.

To learn effectively a student needs: plenty of practice; instant knowledge of whether his or her answers are right or wrong; the ability to set his or her own rate of progress; and most importantly, the satisfaction that comes from successful achievement.

There are other possible educational programs—such as those which use multiple choice answers, and ones based on shapes, such as parts of geometry—which we have not discussed. However, the material we have presented should give you a good point from which to develop your own software.

If you still feel short of ideas, you could send away for catalogues of educational software for any computer. Simply reading a catalogue should be enough to spark more ideas than you can possible realize (in fact, this is one way I get ideas for programs in general, by reading descriptions of what other people's programs do when run).

Now that we've come to the end of this chapter, you should possess a number of simple but effective educational programs. As you extend your collection, either with your own or with commercially-produced software, look for the following points:

- You should not be forced to progress through several screenfulls of preliminary description each time you run the program.
- The amount of material on the screen at any time should be minimized, so that attention is focused on the important details.
- In the presentation of text, different colors should be used with a purpose, as in the DIVISION program.
- It should not be possible to crash the program however you respond to the questions.
- If your answer is wrong, the correct answer must be clearly displayed.
- You should be able to work through the program at your own speed, without information disappearing before you can read it, and without periods of enforced inactivity.

In the final analysis, a good program is one which achieves its objectives, and which is a pleasure to use.

Suggestions for Further Reading

Daniels, J. C. and Diack, Hunter. *The Standard Reading Tests.* Chatto Educational, Ltd. 1958.

Maddison, Alan. *Microcomputers in the Classroom.* London: Hodder and Stoughton, 1982.

Oliva, Ralph A. ed. *Understanding Calculator Math.* Dallas: Texas Instruments Inc., distributed by Tandy/Radio Shack, 1978.

Orwig, Gary W., and Hodges, William S. *The Computer Tutor.* Boston: Little, Brown, Winthrop Publishers, Inc., 1981.

Rogowski, Stephen J. *Problems for Computer Solution.* Creative Computing Press, 1979.

6

Playing Games with Your Timex Sinclair

No matter why you bought your Timex Sinclair, it is likely that you'll spend some of the time with it playing games. It is also likely that you'll soon realize that one of the great thrills of owning a computer is devising your own programs—games or whatever—and making them work.

In this chapter, I'll be looking at a number of games. All of them will be explained in detail, with the intention of passing on some hints on the writing of games which may well be of some help to you when it comes to creating your own programs.

You may be tempted to simply enter the final version of the game, without reading through the material which precedes and follows the listings. If you do this, you'll certainly end up with a program which works, but you'll miss the main point of this chapter. Try to restrain yourself, and follow through the descriptions, line by line, and for those programs which are introduced gradually, entering each part of it when you come to it in the description.

The first two programs, NIGHTFALL and JACK-MAN, are explained in much greater detail than are some of the others. These are the ones you should certainly read carefully, even if you decide to skip the explanations of the later ones. There are many ideas in the first two programs which I think are very useful to know, not only for understanding those particular programs, but for applying to other programming problems.

NIGHTFALL

The first game involves flying an airplane over a city and attempting to reduce the skyscraper to dust. The plane flies across the screen getting lower as it comes to the end of a line. Eventually it crashes into a skyscraper, unless you have first destroyed the buildings.

Our first need is to print up the skyscrapers. This can be done fairly easily by using a FOR/NEXT loop from 0 to 31 (the columns of the screen) with a "nested" loop inside which prints blocks up the screen for the skyscrapers. To make this clear try this program:

```
10 FOR a=0 TO 31
20 FOR b=11 TO 21
30 PRINT AT b,a;"█"
40 NEXT b
50 NEXT a
```

It will print a whole load of skyscrapers of equal length across the screen. Try altering the values of *b* in line 20 to vary the height of the skyscrapers.

However, this routine does not produce a very interesting skyline; it looks more like a large shoe-box than a city. To give the skyscrapers varying heights we need a random factor. Try changing line 20 to:

```
20 FOR B=INT (RND*22) TO 21
```

The skyline will now look much more varied. The routine is now beginning to create something which looks more like a city. However it lacks uniformity. The first routine makes a city that is too uniform, the second a city which is too random. We need a guideline around which a random-factor can work. Rather than let a random-factor rule us, we need to control it. To this end we can bring in a "difficulty factor."

In order to plot a convincing-looking city we need a rough height around which to build skyscrapers. Some will be slightly taller than the average height, some will be smaller, but none will be very much taller or smaller. In the last routine the average height was eleven characters high; but some buildings were 21 characters high, while others were only one high. A difficult game would be where the average height was about 18, since your plane would soon crash into the building. An easier game would be where the average height was, say, five. Your plane would take quite a long time to get to that level and crash into a building. Obviously, on the easy game it would be stupid to have an average height of five and find that one or two buildings were 20 characters high, because the game would no longer be easy.

At the beginning of the game we want to ask the user for a degree of difficulty (for example, in the range of one to nine). With this, we could

build skyscrapers at a rough height guided by the difficulty chosen. Try
the following routine:

```
10 INPUT "difficulty (1-9)",d
20 IF d<1 OR d>9 THEN GO TO 10
30 LET d=12-d
35 CLS
40 FOR a=0 TO 31
50 FOR b=d+INT (RND*d) TO 21
60 PRINT AT b,a; "█"
70 NEXT b
80 NEXT a
90 GO TO 10
```

Type in a number from one to nine and the Timex Sinclair will print up
a fairly realistic skyline. Try putting in a low number and you will find that
the city is accordingly low. What happens when you enter a number
which is outside the range required? Why? Any program you write should
contain a routine to reject invalid input.

People often make a mistake when entering information via the
keyboard, and if unchecked, the error can stop the program completely,
or—if it continues to run—can confuse you with the results it generates. A
single line which checks the range of the number entered can save problems.

If you understand how the program works so far, we are ready to go
on to the next stage: that of producing a moving airplane to fly across the
city.

First of all we need to choose what our plane looks like. Searching
around the keyboard I can't find any symbol which looks even vaguely
like an aircraft of any sort. It looks as though we are going to have to
employ user-defined graphics. Here's a step-by-step way of doing it:

1. Draw a grid of eight by eight squares

2. Fill in squares until you have something which resembles an aircraft
    from the side. Even if it seems a bit square don't worry, as it will
    probably look all right on the screen.
    Here's the one I used:

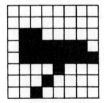

Now go across each row and write down a zero if a square is not
filled in, and a one if it is. For the above character you would get

```
00000000
00000000
01100000
01111110
01111111
00001000
00010000
00100000
```

Each row of zeros and/or ones is called a binary number.

3. Using your Timex Sinclair, go to each row in turn and type:

    PRINT BIN   (the series of zeroes and ones)

    and write down the ordinary number it prints up, alongside the binary
    number you have just typed in. For example, for the third row you
    would type:

    PRINT BIN 01100000

    and the computer would display the number 96. You write this down
    beside the number on the piece of paper, as follows:

    0 1 1 0 0 0 0 0   96

    Do not ignore any trailing zeros as:

    0 1 1 0 0 0 0 0=96

    but

    0 1 1 0 0 0=24

You should now have eight numbers. If you used the above example
you will have the numbers 0, 0, 96, 126, 127, 8, 16 and 32 *in that order*.
Clear your Timex Sinclair (by using NEW) and type:

```
10 DATA [your eight numbers]
20 FOR a=0 TO 7
30 READ b: POKE USR "a"+a,b
40 NEXT a
```

The DATA statement should contain your eight numbers separated
by commas. Run this and nothing seems to happen. However, now get
into graphics mode and type the letter "a," and there is your tiny aircraft.
You can now NEW the program if you wish and the plane will still be
inside the computer ready for use, in fact the only way to get rid of it is to
pull out the plug or define a new character over it. As well as graphic "a"
you can get the plane by using "CHR$ 144". The above method can be
used for any character you want to design of your own.

Armed with the airplane character we can now go on to make it move
across the city and get lower. Type in the last "city-maker" routine and add
the following lines (in line 20, CHR$ 144 represents your graphics-
airplane):

```
 90 LET u=0
100 LET p=0
140 PRINT AT u,p;CHR$ 144
160 LET p=p+1
170 PRINT AT u,p-1;" "
180 IF p=32 THEN LET p=0: LET u
=u+1: BEEP .1,u
190 GO TO 140
```

You will be asked for a "difficulty," and on entering it, you will see a city printed. Then, you will see a little plane fly across the screen and get lower, beeping as it goes (the ever-rising notes are designed to increase the tension). The plane will soon go through a building and continue until it goes off the bottom of the screen and stops with an error message.

What we want now is to have a line that checks where the plane is being printed, and if it finds this is a skyscraper, blows the plane up. For this we need two routines: one to check for a crash, and a routine to print an explosion.

First the crash-check routine—there are two ways of doing this:

Screen$: Replace line 60 with:

```
 60   PRINT AT b,a;INVERSE 1;"X"        (capital X)
```

and line 140 with:

```
140   IF SCREEN$(u,p)="X" THEN STOP
```

SCREEN$ can read letters and therefore the program will stop when the plane hits an X. This means that the skyscraper-printing routine will have to be altered so that INVERSE X's are printed instead of graphic-blocks, which are not read by SCREEN$.

Attr: To use the ATTR function, replace line 60 with:

```
 60   PRINT AT b,a; INK 5; PAPER 0;"graphic-block"
```

and replace line 140 with:

```
140   IF ATTR (u,p)=5 THEN STOP
```

This works by stopping the program whenever the plane comes to *any character* which is cyan on black and is not flashing and has no extra brightness. The disadvantage of this method is that it is a little complicated, and if, in other programs, there are many different characters whizzing all over the place, it gets a bit confusing trying to work out each character's paper color and the like.

If you wanted to stop the program when the plane hit a yellow, flashing blob you would change line 140 to:

```
140   IF ATTR (u,p)=134 THEN STOP
```

Can you see how this works?

128 if the character is flashing, 0 if steady yes:	1 × 128 = 128
64 if the character is extra bright, 0 if not no:	0 × 64 = 0
8 × the paper color (black = 0)	8 × 0 = 0
1 × the ink color (yellow = 6)	1 × 6 = 6
	TOTAL = 134

Out of the two methods, the easiest to use here is SCREEN$, in the form:

```
PRINT AT b,a; INVERSE 1;"X"
IF SCREEN$ (u,p)="X" THEN . . . . . . . . .
```

As there are only two things that the plane will come across, the air and the skyscraper, this function satisfies our requirements. Replace line 140 with:

```
140   IF SCREEN$ (u,p)="X" THEN STOP
```

add line 142:

```
142   PRINT AT u,p; CHR$ 144
```

and not forgetting line 60:

```
60   PRINT AT b,a; INVERSE 1;"X"
```

The program will now STOP when the plane hits a building.

A STOP is a bit boring and unimaginative. What we need is an exciting explosion as the plane shatters. Try the following:

```
200 LET x=p*8: LET y=(21-u)*8
205 FOR a=1 TO 40
207 PLOT x,y
210 DRAW INT (RND*256)-x,INT (R
ND*158)-y
220 BEEP .1,20: BEEP .01,10
230 NEXT a
```

Pick a point on the screen and assign the coordinates to u and p, such as LET u=11: LET p=16. Enter these in directly. Now type: GO TO 200 and press ENTER.

You should see the point on the screen "explode," accompanied by suitable noises. All we have to do now is change line 140 to:

```
140   IF SCREEN$ (u,p)="X" THEN GO TO 200
```

RUN the whole program and you will get:

1. a city plotted up on to the screen,
2. a plane whizzing along getting lower and lower
3. the plane hitting a building and exploding.

Now, read through the program again. Make sure you understand how it works. Now, we're ready to add the final parts. These involve having a bomb which you can drop from the plane to destroy the skyscrapers and prolong your flight, and then dressing the program up to make it look more professional.

Unfortunately, you are unlikely to completely finish this, or any game. No sooner have you SAVEd it and sat back admiring what you believe to be the definitive version, than someone will come along, play it, and give you a great idea on how to improve it.

However, before worrying about any of that, we need to add the bomb bit of the program. For this, we need a *flag*. A flag is an indicator of the state something is in. It is usually given a value of 1 for on, and 0 for off. In this program the flag which we'll call "f," will be equal to one when the bomb is in the air, and zero when it is not. At the beginning we need to assign it to zero as the bomb is not falling. This is how the program should look so far with "f" being set equal to zero:

```
10   INPUT "difficulty (1-9)",d
20   IF d<1 OR d>9 THEN GO TO 10
30   LET d=12-d
35   CLS
40   FOR a=0 TO 31
50   FOR b=d+INT (RND*d) TO 21
60   PRINT AT b,a; INVERSE 1;"X"
70   NEXT b
80   NEXT a
90   LET u=0
100  LET p=0
110  LET f=0
140  IF SCREEN$ (u,p)="X" THEN G
O TO 200
142  PRINT AT u,p;CHR$ 144
160  LET p=p+1
170  PRINT AT u,p-1;"  "
180  IF p=32 THEN LET p=0: LET u
=u+1: BEEP .1,u
190  GO TO 140
200  LET x=p*8: LET y=(21-u)*8
205  FOR a=1 TO 40
207  PLOT x,y
210  DRAW INT (RND*256)-x,INT (R
ND*158)-y
220  BEEP .1,20: BEEP .01,10
230  NEXT a
```

The bomb is "off" (f = 0). What we need is a means of allowing the user to drop a bomb (make f = 1). One easy way would be to add a line like:

```
148 IF INKEY$ <>"" THEN LET f=1
```

INKEY$ holds the character of the key being pressed on the keyboard (it is "empty" if no key is being pressed). The routine changes f to 1 when you press any key, when INKEY$ is not equal to " ". We could change the routine a little so the bomb is only dropped when the zero key is pressed.

To do this you would need:

```
148   IF INKEY$ = "0" THEN LET f=1
```

However, it is easier to play (and remember) if you can press any key to drop the bomb, so we'll leave 148 to allow any key to be pressed.

Next we need two variables representing the position of the bomb on the screen. When the bomb is "off" it is inside the aircraft ready to be dropped:

```
144   IF f=0 THEN LET a=u: LET t=p
      ("a" and "t" are the coordinates of the bomb)
```

We next need a character which looks like a bomb. A full-stop is adequate, but you may prefer to define your own bomb. Using the method outlined earlier, see if you can design a bomb-character. One bomb-shape is as follows:

								0
								0
								0
		■						32
			■	■	■			28
		■						32
								0
								0

The line which defines the character should read:

```
POKE USR "b" +a,b
```

and *not:*

```
POKE USR "a" +a,b
```

as this will blot out the plane-character.

To access this new bomb-character use graphic-b or CHR$ 145. If you prefer the simple life, you can use a full-stop as a bomb. In this case, use a full-stop wherever I have put "CHR$ 145".

With our bomb-shape (or full-stop) at the ready, we are now ready to actually print it. As the bomb is at exactly the same position as the plane when it is not falling (when $f = 0$), we do not want to print it up until it starts falling, or the bomb will blank out the plane. Line 158 will print the bomb:

```
158   IF f=1 THEN PRINT AT a,t; CHR$ 145: BEEP .01,60-a
```

The bomb will now be printed up whenever you press a button. It will not fall however, until you add the following line 155, which blanks out the bomb and adds one onto the variable "a" which in effect moves it down:

```
155   IF f=1 THEN PRINT AT a,t;" ": LET a=a+1
```

Although we now have a falling bomb, it is not a very good one because it carries on down to the bottom and halts the program with an error-code. What is needed is a line which checks whether the bomb has hit a building (similar to line 140), or reached the bottom of the screen.

```
157   IF SCREEN$(a,t)="X" OR a=21 THEN GO TO 300
```

Now we can write a "building-blowing-up" routine at 300:

```
300   FOR a=a TO 21
310   IF RND > .99 THEN GO TO 340
315   BEEP .005,a-20
320   PRINT AT a,t;" "
330   NEXT a
340   LET f=0: GO TO 140
```

All we need now is:

```
235   GO TO 10
```

and we have a continuous game. It is quite difficult to aim and drop the bomb on the buildings you want to destroy.

Here is a complete listing of the game so far:

```
 10  INPUT "difficulty (1-9)",d
 20  IF d<1 OR d>9 THEN GO TO 10
 30  LET d=12-d
 35  CLS
 40  FOR a=0 TO 31
 50  FOR b=d+INT (RND*d) TO 21
 60  PRINT AT b,a; INVERSE 1;"X"
 70  NEXT b
 80  NEXT a
 90  LET u=0
100  LET p=0
110  LET f=0
140  IF SCREEN$ (u,p)="X" THEN G
O TO 200
142  PRINT AT u,p;CHR$ 144
144  IF f=0 THEN LET a=u: LET t=
p
148  IF INKEY$<>"" THEN LET f=1
155  IF f=1 THEN PRINT AT a,t;"
": LET a=a+1
157  IF SCREEN$ (a,t)="X" OR a=2
1 THEN GO TO 300
```

```
 158 IF f=1 THEN PRINT AT a,t;CH
R$ 145: BEEP .01,60-a
 160 LET p=p+1
 170 PRINT AT u,p-1;" "
 180 IF p=32 THEN LET p=0: LET u
=u+1: BEEP .1,u
 190 GO TO 140
 200 LET x=p*8: LET y=(21-u)*8
 205 FOR a=1 TO 40
 207 PLOT x,y
 210 DRAW INT (RND*256)-x,INT (R
ND*158)-y
 220 BEEP .1,20: BEEP .01,10
 230 NEXT a
 235 GO TO 10
 300 FOR a=a TO 21
 310 IF RND>.99 THEN GO TO 340
 315 BEEP .005,a-20
 320 PRINT AT a,t;" "
 330 NEXT a
 340 LET f=0: GO TO 140
```

The game works, but it lacks several things. In its present form there is no color, and are no scoring facilities. Try and fit them into the program (you could use a variable s and add 1 to it every time a character of skyscraper is wiped out by a bomb—around line 300 or so). You will need to print the score at the end of the game. In the final version at the end of this section I have included a "highest score" feature. This is fairly simple to add. Try adding little bits to the program to make it smarter. You could try defining your own skyscraper-character with windows rather than a boring INVERSE "X".

The final version shown here has DATA statements to define the user-defined graphic characters, so that it can be typed in and run as it is.

"FINAL" COLOR VERSION OF NIGHTFALL:

```
   2 LET h=0
   4 IF h=0 THEN GO SUB 1000
   5 LET s=0
  10 PAPER 0: INK 6: BORDER 1
  30 PRINT AT 21,0;"difficulty (
1 to 9) ?": LET d$=INKEY$: IF LE
N d$<>1 OR CODE d$<49 OR CODE d$
>57 THEN GO TO 30
  32 CLS
  35 LET d=12-VAL d$
  40 FOR a=0 TO 31
  50 FOR b=d+INT (RND*d) TO 21
  60 PRINT PAPER 0;AT b,a;CHR$ 1
46
  70 NEXT b
  80 NEXT a
  90 LET u=0
 100 LET p=0
 110 LET f=0
```

```
 130 PRINT AT 21,0;CHR$ 20+CHR$
1+d$+" press any key to bomb"
 140 PRINT AT u,p;: IF PEEK (PEE
K 23684+256*PEEK 23685)=255 THEN
 GO TO 200
 142 PRINT INK 4;CHR$ 144
 144 IF f=0 THEN LET a=u: LET t=
p
 148 IF INKEY$<>"" THEN LET f=1
 155 IF f=1 THEN PRINT AT a,t;"
 ": LET a=a+1: IF a=22 THEN GO TO
 340
 157 PRINT AT a,t;: IF PEEK (PEE
K 23684+256*PEEK 23685)=255 THEN
 GO TO 300
 158 IF f=1 THEN PRINT INK 2;CHR
$ 145: BEEP .01,60-a
 160 LET p=p+1
 170 PRINT AT u,p-1;" "
 180 IF p=32 THEN LET p=0: LET u
=u+1: BEEP .1,u
 185 IF u=22 THEN GO TO 1200
 190 GO TO 140
 200 LET x=p*8: LET y=(21-u)*8
 205 FOR a=1 TO s STEP 10
 207 PLOT x,y
 210 DRAW INK 6; INT (RND*256)-x,
INT (RND*158)-y
 220 BEEP .1,20: BEEP .01,10
 230 NEXT a
 235 GO TO 400
 300 FOR a=a TO 21
 310 IF RND>.99 THEN GO TO 340
 315 BEEP .005,a-20
 320 PRINT AT a,t;" "
 325 LET s=s+1: IF s/250=INT (s/
250) THEN POKE 23624,PEEK 23624+
8
 330 NEXT a
 340 LET f=0: GO TO 140
 400 IF h<s THEN LET h=s
 410 PRINT AT 0,0;"score: ";s,"h
i-score: ";h
 420 GO TO 5
1000 DATA "a",0,0,96,126,127,8,1
6,0,"b",0,0,0,32,28,32,0,0,"c",2
55,153,153,255,255,153,153,255
1005 FOR f=1 TO 3
1007 READ a$
1010 FOR a=0 TO 7
1020 READ b: POKE USR a$+a,b
1030 NEXT a
1045 NEXT f
1050 RETURN
1200 DATA 0,4,7
1210 FOR a=1 TO 3
1215 READ c
1220 FOR b=1 TO 3
1230 BEEP 1/3,c
1240 NEXT b
1250 NEXT a
1260 BEEP 1,12
1270 GO TO 32
```

NIGHTFALL IN PROGRESS

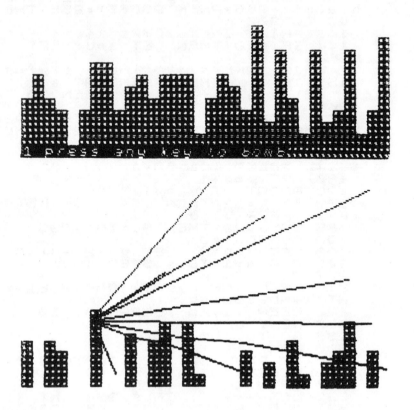

I hope the explanation of this game has given you a few ideas on how games can be developed. We'll be looking at several other games in the rest of this chapter, but not in quite as much detail as NIGHTFALL.

JACK-MAN

This program is based very loosely on DODGEM (with a hint of PAC-MAN), in which the player propels a little car around a maze, scoring points as it runs over dots within the maze, and trying to avoid running head-on into a car "driven" by the computer.

The scenario for JACK-MAN is less gruesome. JACK is a dastardly grape thief within an elaborately-designed French vineyard. The object of the game is to guide Jack around the vineyard to eat as many grapes as possible. At the same time, he must elude the irate farmer.

Here is a plan of the vineyard, complete with grapes:

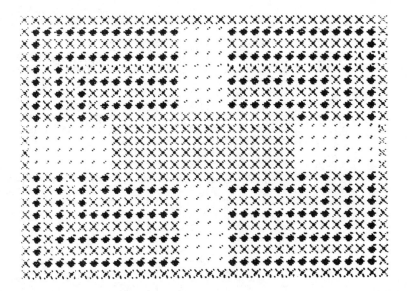

Nearly a third of the final program is taken up by the routine that prints up the vineyard with its different-colored walls and grapes (all the grapes are the same color, as are all the walls, but the grapes are colored differently from the walls). It would be wise to SAVE the routine below, as it is so long, so that you can add to it later rather than have to retype it if you lose it for some reason.

Note that the G's must be entered in the graphics mode.

```
  2 LET h=0
  5 LET e$="Jack"
 10 DATA 60,126,240,224,224,240
,126,60
 12 DATA 0,66,195,195,231,255,1
26,60,60,126,15,7,7,15,126,60
 14 DATA 60,126,255,231,195,195
,66,0,0,0,0,0,60,60,60,60
 16 DATA 60,126,255,255,255,255
,126,60,0,0,0,60,126,60,24,0
 20 DATA 24,60,24,255,24,24,36,
102
 25 FOR a=0 TO 7
 30 FOR b=0 TO 7
 40 READ c
 50 POKE USR CHR$ (144+a)+b,c
 60 NEXT b
 70 NEXT a
 75 LET s=0: LET v=1
 77 LET z=4: LET y=0: PAPER 3:
INVERSE 1
 78 LET f=0
 79 CLS
 80 PRINT INK z;"XXXXXXXXXXXXXX
XXXXXXXXXXXXXXXX"
 90 IF f=1 THEN RETURN
100 PRINT INK z;"X"; INK y;"GGG
```

```
GGGGGGGGGG''''GGGGGGGGGGGGG"; IN
K z;"X"
 110 IF f=1 THEN GO TO 80
 120 PRINT INK z;"X"; INK y;"G";
 INK z;"XXXXXXXXXXXX"; INK y;"''
''"; INK z;"XXXXXXXXXXXX"; INK y
;"G"; INK z;"X"
 130 IF f=1 THEN GO TO 100
 140 PRINT INK z;"X"; INK y;"G";
 INK z;"X"; INK y;"GGGGGGGGGG''
''GGGGGGGGGG"; INK z;"X"; INK y
;"G"; INK z;"X"
 150 IF f=1 THEN GO TO 120
 160 PRINT INK z;"X"; INK y;"G";
 INK z;"X"; INK y;"G"; INK z;"XX
XXXXXXXX"; INK y;"'''''"; INK z;"
XXXXXXXXXX"; INK y;"G"; INK z;"X
"; INK y;"G"; INK z;"X"
 170 IF f=1 THEN GO TO 140
 180 PRINT INK z;"X"; INK y;"G";
 INK z;"X"; INK y;"G"; INK z;"X"
; INK y;"GGGGGGGGG''''GGGGGGGGG"
; INK z;"X"; INK y;"G"; INK z;"X
"; INK y;"G"; INK z;"X"
 190 IF f=1 THEN GO TO 160
 200 PRINT INK z;"X"; INK y;"G";
 INK z;"X"; INK y;"G"; INK z;"X"
; INK y;"G"; INK z;"XXXXXXXX"; I
NK y;"''''''"; INK z;"XXXXXXXX"; I
NK y;"G"; INK z;"X"; INK y;"G";
INK z;"X"; INK y;"G"; INK z;"X"
 210 IF f=1 THEN GO TO 180
 220 PRINT INK z;"X"; INK y;"G";
 INK z;"X"; INK y;"G"; INK z;"X"
; INK y;"G"; INK z;"X"; INK y;"G
GGGGGG''''GGGGGGG"; INK z;"X"; I
NK y;"G"; INK z;"X"; INK y;"G";
INK z;"X"; INK y;"G"; INK z;"X"
 230 IF f=1 THEN GO TO 200
 240 PRINT INK z;"X"; INK y;"G";
 INK z;"X"; INK y;"G"; INK z;"X"
; INK y;"G"; INK z;"X"; INK y;"G
"; INK z;"XXXXXXXXXXXXXXXXXX"; INK
 y;"G"; INK z;"X"; INK y;"G"; IN
K z;"X"; INK y;"G"; INK z;"X"; I
NK y;"G"; INK z;"X"
 250 IF f=1 THEN GO TO 220
 260 FOR a=1 TO 4
 270 PRINT INK z;"X"; INK y;"'''
'''''"; INK z;"XXXXXXXXXXXXXXXXXX";
 INK y;"''''''"; INK z;"X"
 280 NEXT a
 290 LET f=1
 300 GO SUB 240
 305 INVERSE 0
 307 GO SUB 1040
 310 LET u=20
 315 PAPER 0: INK 6
 320 LET p=17
 330 LET du=0
 335 LET lj=4
```

Having assigned starting values to the high score and the like (see the list of variables at the end) and printed up the vineyard, the program jumps to a routine which:

1. prints the "super grape," a flashing grape which scores five points when eaten rather than the usual one point; once eaten by either the farmer or Jack, it moves to another part of the vineyard;
2. plays a little tune. Many arcade games play a tune to start with and after playing the game a number of times, this tune gets on your nerves. If the music irritates you in this program, by all means leave it out. The Timex Sinclair reads the notes for the music from the DATA statement at line 1050.

As the program jumps to this routine whenever a "sheet" is cleared, the high score changes when the score goes beyond it.

On returning from the subroutine most of the other variables used during the game are set to their starting values.

The program then continues on to the main part of the program which sends the action to different subroutines when the player wants to move Jack, or when Jack hits a wall.

The subroutines are as follows:

1. Automatic Jack-moving Routine: This changes the direction and the character of Jack when he hits a wall; that is, if he is moving east and he hits a wall, the program automatically changes his direction so that he is moving north, and changes the character used so that he is also "chomping" northwards. The player has no control over this. Jack is always moving counter-clockwise.

2. Manual Jack-moving Routine: Each row of grapes is closed off by a wall and therefore Jack cannot move across the rows. However there are four gaps where Jack can move to new lines of grapes and/or avoid the oncoming farmer. This routine is utilized when (a) Jack is in a gap and (b) when the player is pressing a key. The routine checks whether the player is trying to move Jack in a valid direction, and if so moves Jack, adjusts the relevant variables and sounds a note to help the user. If the user tries to move Jack illegally, a different note is sounded.

3. Automatic Farmer-moving Routine: This adjusts the farmer's direction when he hits a wall (see Automatic Jack-moving Routine).

4. Manual Farmer-moving Routine: This routine is called when (a) the farmer is in a gap and (b) the farmer is not in the same line of grapes as Jack. Therefore, the farmer is always on par for a collision with Jack. To start off with, however, he can only move across by one, but as Jack clears more and more sheets, the farmer's maneuverability increases and the game becomes more difficult.

5. Sheet Clearing Routine: This is used when Jack has eaten all the grapes, and sets up a new vineyard. It is not so much a subroutine as a series of commands which call up parts of other subroutines.

6. End of Game Routine: This is called when the farmer "hits" Jack. It shrivels Jack up while playing suitable sound-effects and alters the high score, if the player has achieved one, asking for his or her name. It then sends the action back to the beginning (without resetting the high score variable).

7. "Super-grape" Routine: This is called at the beginning of the program but is also called when Jack eats a super-grape. It blanks out the old "super-grape" (by resetting 1$) and then picks a point at random from the screen and checks whether it is a suitable point to place a new "super-grape." If it is not, then it goes back and picks another random point. A suitable point is defined as a point which is

   a.   not on a wall
   b.   not in a gap
   c.   on an ordinary grape
   d.   on a place where Jack has eaten a grape when more than half the grapes have been eaten.

The main program moves Jack and the farmer in their relevant directions and calls up any of the above routines when needed. The subroutines are situated as follows:

Subroutine	Lines
Automatic Jack-moving Routine	1000–1015
Manual Jack-moving Routine	565– 700
Automatic Farmer-moving Routine	1020–1030
Manual Farmer-moving Routine	710– 790
End of Game Routine	800– 900
'Super-grape' Routine	1150–1250

I worked on each routine in turn, and then perfected the game as a whole.

You might find it easier to enter the program if you ask a friend to read out the listing (especially the vineyard-printing routine at the beginning with all its INKs and PAPERs).

When typing in the program, it is imperative that you use graphics G's and not just ordinary G's, or the grapes will not be printed up. You might like to try typing in the part of the program that defines the user-graphics first and then you will see a grape come up whenever you use graphics G.

FINAL LISTING JACK-MAN

```
   2 LET h=0
   5 LET e$="Jack"
  10 DATA 60,126,240,224,224,240
,126,60
  12 DATA 0,66,195,195,231,255,1
26,60,60,126,15,7,7,15,126,60
  14 DATA 60,126,255,231,195,195
,66,0,0,0,0,60,60,60,60
  18 DATA 60,126,255,255,255,255
,126,60,0,6,8,60,126,60,24,0
  20 DATA 24,60,24,255,24,24,36,
102
  25 FOR a=0 TO 7
  30 FOR b=0 TO 7
  40 READ c
  50 POKE USR CHR$ (144+a)+b,c
  60 NEXT b
  70 NEXT a
  75 LET s=0: LET v=1
  77 LET z=4: LET y=0: PAPER 3:
INVERSE 1
  78 LET f=0
  79 CLS
  80 PRINT INK z;"XXXXXXXXXXXXXX
XXXXXXXXXXXXXXXXXXX"
  90 IF f=1 THEN RETURN
 100 PRINT INK z;"X"; INK y;"GGG
GGGGGGGGGG''''GGGGGGGGGGGGGG"; IN
K z;"X"
 110 IF f=1 THEN GO TO 80
 120 PRINT INK z;"X"; INK y;"G";
INK z;"XXXXXXXXXXXX"; INK y;"";
''"; INK z;"XXXXXXXXXXXX"; INK y
;"G"; INK z;"X"
 130 IF f=1 THEN GO TO 100
 140 PRINT INK z;"X"; INK y;"G";
INK z;"X"; INK y;"GGGGGGGGGGG''
''GGGGGGGGGG"; INK z;"X"; INK y
;"G"; INK z;"X"
 150 IF f=1 THEN GO TO 120
 160 PRINT INK z;"X"; INK y;"G";
INK z;"X"; INK y;"G"; INK z;"XX
XXXXXXXX"; INK y;"'''''"; INK z;"
XXXXXXXXXX"; INK y;"G"; INK z;"X
"; INK y;"G"; INK z;"X"
 170 IF f=1 THEN GO TO 140
 180 PRINT INK z;"X"; INK y;"G";
INK z;"X"; INK y;"G"; INK z;"X"
; INK y;"GGGGGGGGG''''GGGGGGGGG"
; INK z;"X"; INK y;"G"; INK z;"X
"; INK y;"G"; INK z;"X"
 190 IF f=1 THEN GO TO 160
 200 PRINT INK z;"X"; INK y;"G";
INK z;"X"; INK y;"G"; INK z;"X"
; INK y;"G"; INK z;"XXXXXXXX"; I
NK y;"'''''"; INK z;"XXXXXXXX"; I
NK y;"G"; INK z;"X"; INK y;"G";
INK z;"X"; INK y;"G"; INK z;"X"
 210 IF f=1 THEN GO TO 180
 220 PRINT INK z;"X"; INK y;"G";
```

```
      INK z;"X";  INK y;"G";  INK z;"X"
    ;  INK y;"G";  INK z;"X";  INK y;"G
    GGGGGG";  "GGGGGGG";  INK z;"X";  I
    NK y;"G";  INK z;"X";  INK y;"G";
    INK z;"X";  INK y;"G";  INK z;"X"
    230 IF f=1 THEN GO TO 200
    240 PRINT INK z;"X";  INK y;"G";
    INK z;"X";  INK y;"G";  INK z;"X"
    ;  INK y;"G";  INK z;"X";  INK y;"G
    ";  INK z;"XXXXXXXXXXXXXXXXX";  INK
    y;"G";  INK z;"X";  INK y;"G";  IN
    K z;"X";  INK y;"G";  INK z;"X";  I
    NK y;"G";  INK z;"X"
    250 IF f=1 THEN GO TO 220
    260 FOR a=1 TO 4
    270 PRINT INK z;"X";  INK y;"''''
    '''''";  INK z;"XXXXXXXXXXXXXXXXX";
    INK y;"'''''''''";  INK z;"X"
    280 NEXT a
    290 LET f=1
    300 GO SUB 240
    305 INVERSE 0
    307 GO SUB 1040
    310 LET u=20
    315 PAPER 0:  INK 6
    320 LET p=17
    330 LET du=0
    335 LET lj=4
    340 LET dp=1
    345 LET lf=4
    350 LET a=10
    355 LET g$="'"
    360 LET t=1
    365 LET l$="'"
    370 LET da=-1
    375 PRINT AT 9,9; PAPER 0; INK
    4; INVERSE 1;"Score: "
    380 LET dt=0
    385 LET q=1
    390 LET c=144
    400 IF INKEY$<>"" THEN BEEP .01
    ,0
    410 PRINT AT u,p; INK 6;CHR$ c
    440 IF SCREEN$ (u+du,p+dp)="X"
    THEN GO TO 1000
    460 PRINT AT a,t; INK 3;g$
    470 IF SCREEN$ (a+da,t+dt)="X"
    THEN GO TO 1020
    490 LET g$=SCREEN$ (a+da,t+dt)
    495 IF ATTR (a+da,t+dt)>128 THE
    N LET g$="'"
    500 IF g$<>"'" THEN LET q=v
    510 IF g$<>"'" AND g$<>"," THEN
    LET g$="G"
    515 LET a=a+da: LET t=t+dt
    517 IF a=ba AND t=rt THEN GO SU
    B 1200
    520 IF SCREEN$ (a,t)="'" AND lj
    <>lf THEN GO SUB 710
    525 PRINT AT a,t;"H"
    530 PRINT AT u,p; INK 3;l$
    540 LET u=u+du: LET p=p+dp
```

```
542 IF ATTR (u,p)=6 THEN GO TO
800
545 LET m=0: LET l$=SCREEN$ (u,
p): IF l$="" THEN LET l$=",": LE
T m=1
547 IF u=ba AND p=rl THEN GO SU
B 1150
550 PRINT AT u,p;"F"
555 IF m=1 THEN LET s=s+1: LET
s2=s2+1: BEEP .005,-10: BEEP .00
5,-5: PRINT AT 9,17;s
557 IF s2>=224 THEN GO TO 1110
560 IF INKEY$="" OR l$="," THEN
GO TO 400
565 LET i$=INKEY$
570 IF CODE INKEY$<53 OR CODE I
NKEY$>56 THEN GO TO 400
580 RESTORE 585
585 DATA du,"6","7",dp,"5","8"
590 FOR i=1 TO 2
600 READ j: READ j$: READ k$
610 IF j=0 AND INKEY$<>j$ AND I
NKEY$<>k$ THEN GO TO 400
620 NEXT i
630 LET u1=u: LET p1=p
640 LET u1=u+((i$="6")-(i$="7")
)*(du=0)*2
650 LET p1=p+((i$="8")-(i$="5")
)*(dp=0)*2
655 LET n=(i$="6")*(dp=1)+(i$="
7")*(dp=-1)+(i$="5")*(du=1)+(i$=
"8")*(du=-1)
660 IF n=0 THEN LET n=-1
665 IF lj+n=0 OR lj+n=5 THEN GO
TO 400
670 LET lj=lj+n
675 PRINT AT u,p; INK 3;l$
680 LET u=u1: LET p=p1
690 PRINT AT u,p;"F"
695 BEEP .01,10
700 GO TO 400
710 IF INT q=0 THEN RETURN
715 LET tf=lf+((lf<lj)-(lf>lj))
720 LET q=q-1
730 LET o=((lf>lj)*(da=-1)+((lf<l
j)*(da=1)
740 IF o=0 THEN LET o=-1*(dt=0)
745 LET o=o*2
750 LET t=t+o
760 LET o=((lf>lj)*(dt=1)+((lf<lj
)*(dt=-1)
765 LET lf=tf
770 IF o=0 THEN LET o=-1*(da=0)
775 LET o=o*2
780 LET a=a+o
790 RETURN
800 RESTORE 900
805 FOR a=1 TO 4
810 READ b$: READ r
820 PRINT AT u,p;b$
830 BEEP 1,r
840 NEXT a
```

```
 850 FOR a=1 TO 64
 860 BEEP .01,25
 870 NEXT a
 872 PRINT AT 17,11;"GAME  OVER"
 875 IF h<s THEN INPUT "You have
 attained the hi-score: Please t
ype in your name and      press E
NTER. ";e$: IF LEN e$>11 THEN PR
INT AT v,p-5;"Too long.......":
GO TO 800
 880 IF h<s THEN LET h=s
 885 IF INKEY$="" THEN GO TO 885
 890 GO TO 75
 900 DATA "F",30,"E",20,".",10,"
 ",0
1000 IF du=0 THEN LET du=-dp: LE
T dp=0: LET c=c+1: GO TO 420
1010 IF dp=0 THEN LET dp=du: LET
 du=0: LET c=c+1: IF c=148 THEN
LET c=144
1015 GO TO 420
1020 IF da=0 THEN LET da=dt: LET
 dt=0: GO TO 515
1030 IF dt=0 THEN LET dt=-da: LE
T da=0: GO TO 515
1040 RESTORE 1050
1042 LET s2=0
1045 GO SUB 1200
1050 DATA 7,1,7,.5,7,.5,10,1,12,
1,14,.5,12,1.5,10,1.5,12,.5,7,1,
7,.5,7,.5,10,1,12,1,7,2
1055 DATA 7,1,7,1,10,1,12,1,14,.
5,12,1.5,10,1,12,1,7,1,7,1,5,.5,
4,1.5,0,2
1060 FOR a=1 TO 26
1070 READ w: READ x
1080 BEEP x/10,w
1090 NEXT a
1095 IF h<s THEN LET h=s
1100 PRINT AT 11,9; PAPER 4; INK
 0;"Hi-score: ";h;AT 12,9;"by ";
e$
1105 RETURN
1110 LET v=v+RND
1120 GO TO 77
1150 FOR d=24 TO 0 STEP -1
1155 BEEP .01,d
1160 NEXT d
1165 BEEP .1,36
1170 LET s=s+5
1180 LET l$="."
1200 LET ba=INT (RND*20)+1
1210 LET rl=INT (RND*29)+1
1220 LET b$=SCREEN$ (ba,rl)
1230 IF b$="'" OR b$="X" OR (b$=
"." AND s2<112) OR (ba>8 AND ba<
13) THEN GO TO 1200
1240 PRINT AT ba,rl; FLASH 1; IN
K 5; PAPER 0;"G"
1245 IF s>=112 THEN LET s2=s2+1
1250 RETURN
```

JACK-MAN IN PROGRESS:

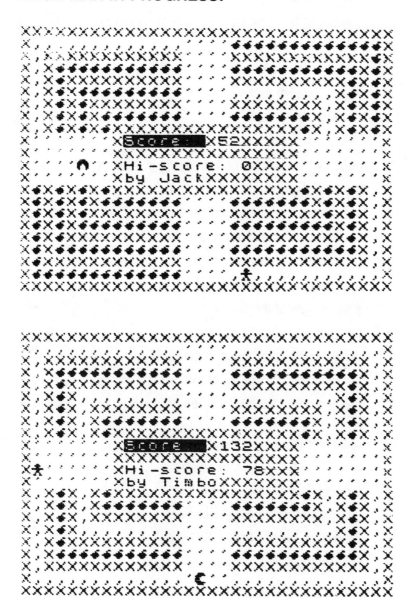

Variables used in Jack-Man

h	highest score so far
e$	name of person who attained the highest score so far
a	control variable for various FOR/NEXT loops
b	control variable for FOR/NEXT loop
c	READs user-defined graphics data

s	present score
v	number of lines the farmer can jump per gap
z	INK color of the walls
y	INK color of the grapes
f	flag for display routine
u	y coordinate of Jack
p	x coordinate of Jack
du	direction down or up of Jack (can be −1, 0 or +1)
lj	the line of grapes Jack is in (1−4)
dp	the direction left or right of Jack (see du)
lf	the line of grapes the farmer is in (see lj)
a	y coordinate of the farmer
g$	the character that blanks out the farmer
t	x coordinate of the farmer
l$	the character that blanks out Jack
da	the direction up or down of the farmer (see du)
dt	the direction left or right of the farmer (see dp)
q	the number of lines jumped by the farmer for this particular gap
c	character used to print Jack
ba	y coordinate of the "super-grape"
rl	x coordinate of the "super-grape"
m	flag for whether a grape has been eaten
i	control variable in FOR/NEXT loop
j	READs legal directions in "Manual Jack-moving Routine"
j$ k$	READs legal character in "Manual Jack-moving Routine"
u1 p1	temporary values of the coordinates of Jack while the "Manual Jack-moving Routine" is checking for a legal move
n	alters the variable that stores the line that Jack is in
o	direction the farmer needs to move in to be aligned with Jack
b$	READs characters printed that shrivel up Jack when "eaten"
r	READs pitch of notes played while Jack is shriveled up

s2	number of grapes eaten so far on this particular sheet
w	READs pitch of notes which play the opening tune
x	READs duration of notes which play the opening tune
i$	key pressed that triggers off the "Manual Jack-moving Routine"

Variables that READ data are those situated within FOR/NEXT loops and are therefore constantly changing values.

POETRY

The first two games we've looked at in this chapter have been moving graphic games, in which player interaction consists of making decisions regarding which keys to press to change the position of objects on the screen.

"Player interaction" *during* the next game is zero, apart from sitting back and admiring the output of the program. The program is designed, firstly, to be entered just as it is, to see it in action. Then, the most enjoyable part begins when you add your own words to the long vocabulary DATA statements between lines 200 and 320.

Here are a few verses of poetry produced by the program in its listed form:

```
THE CHILD PRAYED SOFTLY
    IN THE FOREST,
PLEADING FOR A NEED
    TO SHARE THE MOON...
WATCHING THEN IN CRYING
    ...WATCHING, BLAMING.

THE GIRL SANG SADLY
    IN THE EVENING,
ASKING FOR A WISH
    TO MOVE THE LOVE...
WATCHING THEN IN LAUGHING
    ...WOND'RING, GRASPING.

THE MARTYR CRIED QUICKLY
    IN THE FORECOURT,
CRYING FOR A TORCH
    TO STEAL THE LIGHT...
PASSING NOW IN FADING
    ...GETTING, STARTING.

THE MAN PLEADED QUIETLY
    IN THE DARK,
LOOKING FOR A WISH
    TO PUSH THE SUN...
GETTING AS IN GIVING
    ...SPEAKING, NOTHING.
```

```
THE PROPHET SCREAMED QUIETLY
     IN THE DARK WOODS,
STARING FOR A GATE
     TO FACE THE HATE..
WOND'RING AS IN GRASPING
     ...TREMBLING, DARING.

THE ECHO PRAYED FAINTLY
     IN THE FOREST,
LOOKING FOR A PATH
     TO MOVE THE SUN...
SHAKING NOW IN GIVING
     ...GETTING, GRASPING.
```

and here is the program listing:

POETRY

```
  10 REM Poetry
  20 DIM A$(13,12): DIM B(13)
  30 RANDOMIZE : GO TO 90
  40 FOR M=1 TO 13
  50 RESTORE 190+10*M
  60 FOR G=1 TO RND*10+1: READ B
$: NEXT G: LET A$(M)=B$
  70 LET B(M)=LEN B$: NEXT M
  80 RETURN
  90 POKE 23692,0
 100 FOR H=1 TO 10
 110 GO SUB 40
 120 PRINT '"THE ";A$(1)( TO B(1
));" ";A$(2)( TO B(2));" ";A$(3)
( TO B(3)),"    IN THE ";A$(4)( T
O B(4));","
 130 PRINT A$(5)( TO B(5));" FOR
 A ";A$(6)( TO B(6)),"    TO ";A$
(7)( TO B(7));" THE ";A$(8)( TO
B(8));".."
 140 PRINT A$(9)( TO B(9));" ";A
$(10)( TO B(10));" IN ";A$(11)(
TO B(11))
 150 PRINT TAB 5;"...";A$(12)( T
O B(12));", ";A$(13)( TO B(13));
".
 160 PAUSE 200
 170 INK RND*6
 180 NEXT H
 190 STOP
 200 DATA "MAN","BOY","WOMAN","C
HILD","SHADOW","ECHO","GIRL","ST
ALLION","PROPHET","MARTYR"
 210 DATA "SANG","WAITED","SAID"
,"SCREAMED","CRIED","PLEADED","P
RAYED","STOOD","FELL","STUMBLED"
 220 DATA "SADLY","GLADLY","SLOW
LY","FAINTLY","MADLY","HUMBLY","
LOUDLY","SOFTLY","QUIETLY","QUIC
KLY"
 230 DATA "DARK","DOORWAY","GATE
WAY","MORNING","EVENING","FORECO
URT","ARCHWAY","DARK WOODS","CAN
YON","FOREST"
```

```
240 DATA "LOOKING","SEARCHING",
"HOPING","TOUCHING","REACHING",
STARING","ASKING","PLEADING","WA
ITING","CRYING"
250 DATA "WAY","PATH","STEP","S
IGN","WISH","NEED","TORCH","DOOR
","GATE","DEATH"
260 DATA "REACH","TOUCH","MOVE"
,"STEAL","SHARE","TURN","TWIST",
"FACE","PUSH","BLAME"
270 DATA "MOON","SEA","NIGHT","
PAIN","LOVE","HATE","SUN","FEAR"
,"JOY","LIGHT","DAY"
280 DATA "TAKING","WATCHING","P
ASSING","BLAMING","GETTING","SHA
KING","TREMBLING","WOND'RING","T
EACHING","SPEAKING"
290 DATA "HEART","HOW","WHY","D
OWN","THROUGH","FOR","THEN","JUS
T","AS","NOW"
300 DATA "NOTHING","GIVING","FA
DING","DARING","STARTING","LAUGH
ING","CRYING","BLAMING","CARING"
,"GRASPING"
310 DATA "TAKING","WATCHING","P
ASSING","BLAMING","GETTING","SHA
KING","TREMBLING","WOND'RING","T
EACHING","SPEAKING"
320 DATA "NOTHING","GIVING","FA
DING","DARING","STARTING","LAUGH
ING","CRYING","BLAMING","CARING"
,"GRASPING"
```

It is fairly easy to write poetry programs for a computer, if you follow a simple procedure. The trick is to write a verse of poetry of your own, work out what parts of speech are used in this, and then get the computer to randomly choose words of the correct type to fill designated spaces within the program.

This particular program was written by first creating the following, not very brilliant, verse:

> THE *EAGLE FLEW SWIFTLY*
> IN THE *CLOUDS,*
> SEARCHING FOR A WAY
> TO *TOUCH* THE *SKY* . . .
> *FLYING THEN* IN *CRYING*
> . . . *RUSHING, MOVING*

Next a number of lists of words was built up which would take the place of the words in italics. These words are in the DATA statements from line 200.

Once this is done, the actual program construction is very simple. Line 20 dimensions two arrays, one to hold the word when it is selected, and one to hold the length of that word. Because there are thirteen words to be added to each verse, a loop of one to 13 (line 40) is used. The word

RESTORE means the computer goes back to the beginning of a set of DATA items before READing them. The Timex Sinclair allows you to selectively RESTORE, that is to RESTORE from a specific line. Line 50 RESTOREs the whole of the line whose number is given by 190 + 10*M. This ensures that line 60, which chooses one of the next ten words randomly, always starts its count at the beginning of the correct set of words. Line 70 sets the element of the array B to the length of the word.

Line 90, where the program proper starts, POKEs 23692 with zero. This ensures that the screen automatically scrolls when it is full, rather than stopping with the query "scroll?". Line 100 controls the loop which counts the number of verses the computer writes. In its present form, the Timex Sinclair will write ten verses, but there is no reason why you should not change it to as many or as few as you wish.

We've already discussed the subroutine starting from line 40, which is called from line 110. This selects the words to be used in the verse, loads those words into elements of the array A$ and their lengths into the array B.

Lines 120 to 150 print out the poem. We need the somewhat inelegant (TO B(1)) after each element of the string array is listed to ensure that the trailing spaces (which always fill up a string array to its full length on the Timex Sinclair) are not printed. Without this mechanism, the poems would look very strange indeed on the screen.

There is a pause (of about four seconds) after each verse has been printed, the INK color is changed randomly (line 170) and the computer goes back to print its next verse.

As I said at the beginning of the discussion on this program, the enjoyable part of using it comes when you start substituting your own words for those in the DATA statements given. Once you've done this successfully, you may well want to write an entire poetry program from scratch, starting with a completely different model poem.

METEORS

In this game you are a scout ship flying through space when you suddenly find yourself in a meteor storm. You have to dodge the meteors for as long as possible. Fortunately, there are a number of fuel dumps within the storm, and you can refuel your ship simply by running into them (isn't modern technology wonderful).

You'll recall that in the POETRY program (line 90) we POKEd 23692 with zero to stop the Timex Sinclair scrolling 22 lines, and then stopping to ask "scroll?". We'll do the same in this program which essentially places you near the center of the screen, and then scrolls the universe up around you. The neatest way to get the computer to scroll continuously is to print a NEWLINE character at the bottom of the screen, which then scrolls up to make room for this "new line." The NEWLINE character is 13 (CHR$ 13).

You use the graphics letters shown in the REM statements to represent the symbols. Although you will not see the symbols come up immediately, once lines 5–70 have been run, the graphic letters will have been converted to the user-graphics defined in that part of the program. Again, you may wish to try running these lines first, so that, for example, a meteor will appear every time you press graphic B.

The fuel gauge is stored as a string, decreasing by one pixel's breadth every time a key is pressed and the ship thrusts to the right (it automatically drifts to the left if you don't touch a key). Hyperspacing (which moves your ship to a random point across—for use in emergencies only as you may materialize onto a meteor) uses up a chunk of fuel. If you get low on fuel you can drift (which does not use up fuel), but beware, hanging on the left-hand side of the screen means that you lose points rather than gain them. You refuel by hitting a blue gas pump (recognized by the fact that it is blue). You blow up if you run out of fuel or hit a meteor. The explosion is generated the same way as in NIGHTFALL. The meteors get thicker every 500 points. As with NIGHTFALL, the bigger the score, the bigger the explosion. You hyperspace by pressing the space key; any other key moves you to the right.

You might like to improve the game by adding facilities for firing (perhaps at enemy ships also caught in the meteor storm and appearing from time to time).

PROGRAM LISTING: METEORS

```
 5 LET h=0
10 LET u=11
20 LET p=16
22 LET s=0
25 IF h>0 THEN GO TO 80
30 DATA "a",255,66,66,36,24,24
,24,0,"b",60,126,255,255,255,255
,126,60
32 DATA "c",0,60,126,126,126,1
26,60,0,"d",0,0,24,60,60,24,0,0
33 DATA "m",12,6,50,74,74,122,
122,122
35 FOR b=1 TO 5
37 READ a$
40 FOR a=0 TO 7
50 READ c: POKE USR a$+a,c
60 NEXT a
70 NEXT b
72 DATA 255,127,63,31,15,7,3,1
74 FOR a=0 TO 7: READ c
76 FOR b=0 TO 7: POKE USR CHR$
(a+101)+b,c
```

```
  78 NEXT b: NEXT a
  80 BORDER 0: PAPER 0: INK 6: C
LS
  82 LET a$="█████████████████"
  84 LET sl=16
  86 LET sa=148
  90 REM for Y use graphics A
 100 REM          ●          graphics B
 110 REM          ▪          graphics C
 120 REM          ·          graphics D
 125 REM          @          graphics M
 130 IF SCREEN$ (u,p)<>" " THEN
GO TO 200
 132 PRINT INK 4;AT u,p;"Y"
 135 POKE 23692,255
 137 LET s=s+1: PRINT AT 0,0;s
 139 PRINT AT 0,10;"fuel: "; INK
(sl>=25)*-1+6;TAB sl;a$
 140 FOR a=1 TO s/500+1: PRINT I
NK 2;AT 21,INT (RND*32);CHR$ (14
5+INT (RND*3)): NEXT a
 141 IF RND>.95 THEN PRINT INK 5
;AT 21,INT (RND*31);"@"
 142 IF INKEY$<>"" THEN LET sa=s
a+1: IF sa=156 THEN LET sl=sl+1
: LET a$=a$(2 TO ): LET sa=148
 143 IF sl=31 AND sa=148 THEN GO
TO 200
 144 LET a$(1)=CHR$ sa
 147 IF sl>=25 THEN BEEP .007,sl
 150 PRINT AT u,p;" "
 155 IF INKEY$=" " THEN LET p=IN
T (RND*32): IF LEN a$<=1 THEN GO
TO 200: LET a$=a$(2 TO ): LET s
l=sl+1
 160 PRINT AT 21,0;CHR$ 13
 170 LET p=p-(p>0)+(INKEY$<>"")*
2*(p<31)
 175 IF p=0 THEN LET s=s-2*(s>0)
: BEEP .01,s/20
 180 GO TO 130
 200 IF ATTR (u,p)=5 THEN LET a$
="█████████████████": LET sl=16: P
RINT AT u,p;"*": FOR a=-sl TO 30
: BEEP .01,a: NEXT a: GO TO 132
 202 LET x=p*8: LET y=(21-u)*8
 205 INK 3
 207 FOR c=1 TO s/10
 210 PLOT x,y
 220 LET a=INT (RND*256): LET b=
INT (RND*158)
 230 DRAW a-x,b-y
 235 IF RND>.85 THEN BEEP .01,20
 240 NEXT c
 250 INK 6
 260 BEEP 1,20
 265 IF h<s THEN LET h=s
 270 PRINT AT 21,0;"score: ";s," 
hi-score: ";h
 280 PRINT AT 0,0;"press any key
"
 290 IF INKEY$="" THEN GO TO 290
 300 GO TO 10
```

SAMPLE RUN: METEORS

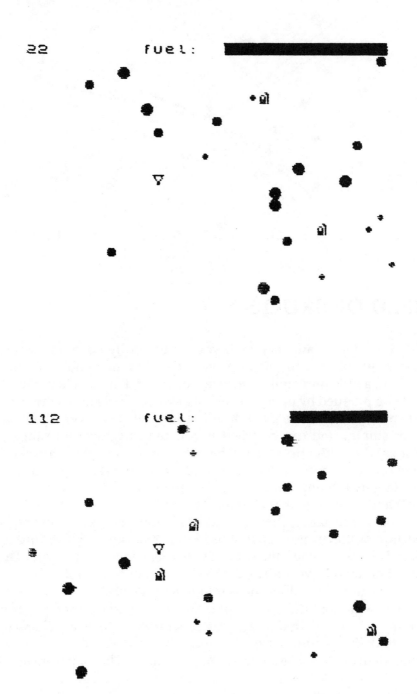

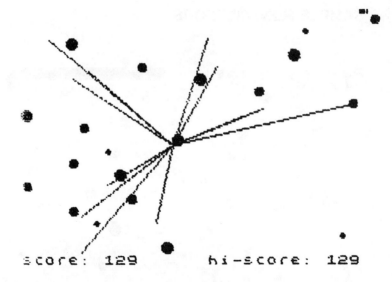

score: 129   hi-score: 129

FIELD OF SKULLS

With a fearsome name like that, you could hardly hope this would be a pleasant game. It is simple to play, but almost impossible to win.

You, a little humanlike creature (see the end of line 140 in the listing), are being pursued by up to ten flashing skulls. They know where you are, and spend most of the game heading for you. However, the skulls are rather stupid, and can be killed if you can lure them into the colored oblongs which litter the screen. The only way you can get them to do this is to get on the opposite side of the oblong from the skulls. As they pursue you, they will bump blindly into the oblongs ("they only have eyes for you") and vanish, with a cheerful "bleep."

You move using the "5," "6," "7" and "8" keys, moving in the direction of the arrows above those keys. You cannot move through the colored oblong patches, but contact with them does not hurt you. The only thing that can hurt you is a skull. The game ends when a skull gets you, or you manage to lure all of them into oblong death.

You will recall the way graphics were defined in other games in this chapter. It can be wasteful to have a separate loop for every character you wish to define, and more than one can be defined within a single loop, although the process can become most complex. The loop from line 400 to 430 defines both the human and the skulls. The DATA statement (line 440) contains the graphics information for both characters, with the information for the human and the skulls interwoven. Graphics "A" becomes the human, "B" becomes the skulls, so you need to put a graphics "B" at the end of line 70, and a graphics "A" at the end of 140 and 270.

FIELD OF SKULLS

```
  10 REM FIELD OF SKULLS
  20 GO SUB 310: REM VARIABLES
  30 FOR B=1 TO 10
  40 IF A(B,1)=1 THEN GO SUB 220
  50 PRINT AT C(B,2),C(B,3);" "
  60 IF A(B,1)<>1 THEN GO TO 160
  70 PRINT AT A(B,2),A(B,3); INK
B/2; FLASH 1;"☻"
  80 LET C(B,2)=A(B,2): LET C(B,
3)=A(B,3)
  90 LET N=N-(INKEY$="5" AND N>0
)+(INKEY$="8" AND N<31)
 100 IF A(B,2)>M THEN LET A(B,2)
=A(B,2)-1
 110 LET M=M+(INKEY$="6" AND M<1
9)-(INKEY$="7" AND M>0)
 120 IF A(B,2)<M THEN LET A(B,2)
=A(B,2)+1
 130 IF SCREEN$ (M,N)="X" THEN L
ET M=X: LET N=Y
 140 PRINT AT X,Y;" ";AT M,N;"☆"
 150 IF A(B,3)<N THEN IF A(B,3)<
28 THEN LET A(B,3)=A(B,3)+INT (4
*RND)
 160 LET X=M: LET Y=N
 170 IF A(B,3)>N THEN IF A(B,3)>
3 THEN LET A(B,3)=A(B,3)-INT (4*
RND)
 180 NEXT B
 190 IF SCORE<10 THEN GO TO 30
 200 PRINT AT 2,0; FLASH 1; BRIG
HT 1; INK 2; PAPER 6;" YOU HAVE
BEATEN THE SKULLS!!!!!"
 210 BEEP .008,60-120*RND: GO TO
210
 220 REM ▉ CHECK SKULLS ▉
 230 IF SCREEN$ (A(B,2),A(B,3))=
"X" THEN LET A(B,1)=0: FOR H=1 T
O 10: BEEP .01,5*H: BEEP .01,50-
5*H: NEXT H: LET SCORE=SCORE+1:
PRINT AT 2,22; FLASH 1; BRIGHT 1
; INK 4;"SCORE> ";SCORE
 240 IF A(B,2)=M AND A(B,3)=N TH
EN PRINT AT C(B,2),A(B,3);" ": G
O TO 260
 250 RETURN
 260 REM ▉ END OF GAME ▉
 270 PRINT AT A(B,2),A(B,3); FLA
SH 1; BRIGHT 1; INK 2;"☆"
 280 BEEP .01,RND*20+40
 290 GO TO 280
 300 STOP
 310 REM ▉ ASSIGN VARIABLES ▉
 320 LET SCORE=0
 330 DIM A(10,3): DIM C(10,3)
 340 FOR B=1 TO 10
 350 LET A(B,1)=1
 360 LET A(B,2)=10+INT (RND*9)
 370 LET A(B,3)=10+INT (RND*19)
```

```
 380 LET C(B,2)=A(B,2): LET C(B,
3)=A(B,3)
 390 NEXT B
 400 FOR J=0 TO 7
 410 READ A: READ B
 420 POKE USR "A"+J,A: POKE USR
"B"+J,B
 430 NEXT J
 440 DATA 28,60,28,126,73,90,127
,126,8,60,20,36,34,60,65,24
 450 LET M=INT (RND*3)+9
 460 LET N=30-INT (RND*30)
 470 LET X=M: LET Y=N
 480 PAPER 7: BORDER 7: CLS
 490 INVERSE 1
 500 FOR G=1 TO 12
 510 PRINT INK G/2;AT RND*16+4,R
ND*26+4;"XX"
 520 NEXT G
 530 INVERSE 0
 540 RETURN
```

PART OF TWO RUNS OF FIELD OF SKULLS:

SCORE> 1

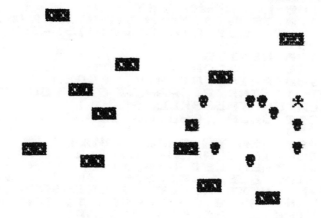

YOU HAVE BEATEN THE SKULLS!!!!!

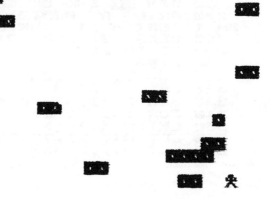

BREAKOUT

The aim of BREAKOUT is to knock out as many bricks as you can at the top of the screen, using a bat at the bottom of the screen which you can move left and right to bounce a ball. If you miss the ball, the game ends.

The game is in five parts:

1. Print up the bricks to be destroyed.
2. Move the bat when required.
3. Bounce the ball when it hits the edge of the screen.
4. Score points for knocking out bricks.
5. End the game if the bat misses the ball.

Part 1 is easy and needs no explanation. Part 2 reads the key being pressed from the keyboard and alters the variables of the bat location accordingly. It also checks to make sure the bat is not going off the edges of the screen.

It does all this in one line using the Timex Sinclair's logic which dictates that if a statement is true it is given a value of one, and if false, zero, therefore: (INKEY$="5") is equal to one when the "5" key is pressed, zero when it is not.

So, where p is the x coordinate of the bat, we can use the following expression:

```
LET P=P+((INKEY$="8")*(P<26)-(INKEY$="5")*
(P>0))*2
```

When INKEY$ equals "5," (INKEY$="8") equals zero so nothing is added on to p (since $p + 0 \times 1 = p + 0 = p$), but when p is bigger than zero (p is greater than 0)=1, then $1 \times 1 \times 2 = 2$ is taken away from p. If p is equal to zero, $1 \times 0 \times 2 = 2$ is taken away from p. This is a very useful method of moving things from left to right. Just remember that an expression on its own inside a pair of brackets, for example ($a + b = c$), is taken as being equal to one if it is true, and zero if false, so ($6 + 6 = 12$) equals one, but ($9 \times 2 = 81$) equals zero.

Part 3, which bounces the ball off a wall, just reverses the sign of the "direction" variable of the ball. If the ball has +1 added to it to make it move (to the right) and hits a wall, the variable is multiplied by –1, and the ball will have –1 added to it (to move it left). Part 3 also "blips" so that you can hear that the ball has hit a wall.

Part 4 uses the ATTR function to see when the ball demolishes a brick. Since all the bricks are yellow, a point is scored every time the ball comes across anything yellow.

Part 5 uses SCREEN$. The bat is made up of capital "X"s so that when the ball comes to the bottom of the screen, it checks whether it is on an "X," and if not it ends the game.

When the ball hits the bat, it bounces off at a random angle (but never straight up). Some angles are quite easy to hit back, but others are wider and are hard to judge. These also give the impression that the game is running more quickly.

There are various changes you could make to the program if you wish. You could try changing it so that the ball sometimes bounces randomly off an odd brick rather than just ploughing through the whole lot. There is no high score factor in the game, and it may be good practice for you to add one. There are no user-defined graphics. Problems occur if you use a graphic bat due to SCREEN$ (see NIGHTFALL), but you could get over them by using the methods given. A graphic ball should not present too many difficulties. You might like to design your own bricks— they can be any shape in this program as long as they are yellow (for ATTR to work). They do not even have to be all the same shape—you could have randomly shaped bricks.

Remember, the aim of the game is to knock out all the bricks at the top of the screen by bouncing the ball off the bat, which you can move at the bottom of the screen. Keys "5" and "8" move the bat left and right respectively. The game ends when the bat misses the ball. You score one point for each brick knocked out.

PROGRAM LISTING: BREAKOUT

```
  10 BORDER 0: PAPER 0: INK 0
  20 CLS
  25 INK 6
  30 FOR a=1 TO 6
  40 FOR b=0 TO 31
  50 PRINT "■";
  60 NEXT b
  70 NEXT a
  80 LET u=21
  90 LET p=14
 140 INK 4
 150 LET a=u
 155 LET s=0
 160 LET t=p+1
 162 LET dt=(INT (RND*5)+1)/(INT
(RND*5)+1)
 165 LET da=-1
 170 PRINT AT u,p; INVERSE 1;"XX
XX"
 172 PRINT AT 11,0;s
 173 IF INKEY$="z" THEN COPY
 175 PRINT AT a,t;"  "
 180 LET a=a+da
 190 LET t=t+dt
 195 IF a=0 OR a=21 OR t<=0 OR t
>=31 THEN GO TO 240
 197 IF ATTR (a,t)=6 THEN LET s=
s+1
 200 PRINT AT a,t; INVERSE 1; IN
K 1;"O"
 210 PRINT AT u,p;"       "
 220 LET p=p+((INKEY$="8")*(p<26
)-(INKEY$="5")*(p>0))*2
 225 LET p=p+(INKEY$="8")*(p=26)
-(INKEY$="5")*(p=25)
 230 GO TO 170
 240 IF a=21 AND SCREEN$ (a,t)="
X" THEN GO TO 162
```

```
250 IF a=21 THEN GO TO 310
260 IF t<=0 THEN LET t=ABS t: L
ET dt=-dt
270 IF t>=31 THEN LET t=31: LET
dt=-dt
280 BEEP .1,-10
290 IF a=0 THEN LET da=1
300 GO TO 200
310 PRINT AT a,t; INK 2;"█"
320 BEEP 1,15
330 IF INKEY$<>"" THEN GO TO 33
0
340 IF INKEY$="" THEN GO TO 340
350 RUN
```

GAMBLIN' FEVER

This program, a variation of the fruit machine or slot machine idea, makes effective use of user-defined graphics (in blocks of 4) to create a slot machine which positively bristles with features. The program listing gives no hint of how effective this looks when running on a color television.

The concept of the game is simple: You start off with $50 in front of a slot machine which has four "windows," behind which reels revolve. The reels contain a random, equally distributed mix of 3 symbols—BELL, CHERRY and APPLE. You press ENTER and the reels start spinning, eventually coming to rest with symbols showing through the windows. If three of them are the same, you win $35. If all four of them are the same, you win $100.

The game continues until you "break the bank" (make $500 or more), or go broke. Each spin costs you $5.00 and this is automatically deducted from your money total, which is shown in the top right hand corner of the screen.

From time to time, a HOLD mechanism comes into play. The word HOLD starts flashing, and you can then keep any of the windows fixed for the next spin. You do this by entering the number of the window (they are numbered from left to right), then pressing ENTER. You can hold any number (or none) you like, and you indicate that you've finished selecting the numbers you wish to hold by pressing ENTER, without preceding it with a number.

There is one more feature. The BELL is the most valuable symbol (which is why it is worth HOLDing BELLs when they come up). Two BELLs next to each other (except when there are four BELLs) are worth a bonus of $15, so if you have three BELLs, instead of making the normal $35 for three symbols the same, you make $50. If you do not have three in a row, but there are two bells next to each other, you'll get the $15 bonus automatically. The program does not highlight this bonus, but quietly adds it to your total.

This program is designed to act as a framework within which you can add whatever features you like. Extra symbols could be one idea, different sounds, a NUDGE mechanism—the development of the program is only limited by your imagination.

You'll read in the chapter on improving your programs a suggestion for working out, in advance and in writing, the major sections you'll need in a program, and then starting off by assigning the major ideas to separate subroutines. The subroutines can be called from a master subroutine call loop at the beginning of the program. This is what we have done in this case.

If you look at the beginning of the listing, you'll see there are three subroutine calls, followed by a GO TO 40, which takes you back to the second and third subroutines repeatedly. The first subroutine (from line 720) assigns the starting variables, and defines the graphics for the symbols. The second, which is called throughout the program, spins the reels. This subroutine starts at line 290, and it calls a further subroutine (from line 210) a number of times (8, in fact) during each round of the game. The final subroutine, which is only called if the random number generated (in line 50) is greater than 45, brings the HOLD option into play.

You can see from the beginning of the listing how the program was written. The first thing I did was work out what I would need (initialization, a spin routine, and a HOLD routine), and then wrote the lines to call up subroutines. The program was renumbered at the end, but initially I left a lot of room between the subroutines, starting the initialization one at 9000, the SPIN at 8000, the PRINT REELS (which is called within SPIN) at 6000 and the HOLD at 3000.

You'll see that the program is clearly broken down into sections by the strips of asterisks in REM statements. This makes it relatively easy to work out which part of the program is in charge of which task, and should make it easy for you to modify if you decide to. You can, for example, change the PRINT REELS section (210 to 280) without changing anything else at all.

Working in this way, and applying the other suggestions given in Chapter 9, A Guide to Better Programming, should help you write programs which not only work with a minimum of debugging but are sufficiently clear to be readily understood when you return to them after a break.

We'll look at the program section by section now, and outline what each is doing.

We've already discussed the first section (lines 10 to 60) which cycle is called by the program through the subroutine. We'll look at the subroutines in the order in which they are called, rather than the order in which they appear in the program, as this makes it easier to understand what tasks they are carrying out.

The first subroutine starts at line 720, and as the REM statement points out, this is for variables and graphics. It is always a good idea to assign the variables at the end of the program, not only to ensure that the program runs as fast as possible, but to give you a lot of room to add extra variables if you discover, as the program writing is under way, that additional ones are needed.

The variable MONEY, fairly obviously, holds the money you have, and starts off with a value of 50. Line 760 dimensions four arrays, the first two (the string arrays) to hold the user-defined graphics *and* their colors (I'll explain this shortly), the second two to hold the numbers created for each "spin of the reels" (A), and to hold your wishes regarding HOLD(Q).

The routines from 770 to 1030 define the graphics, calling on the DATA statements from line 1150 onward. Lines 840 and 850 add together the four quarters of the apple, along with the control character (CHR$ 16) for INK and the character for red (CHR$ 2). This ensures that the statement PRINT A$(1) for example will print the top half of the apple, in red, without the need for PRINT INK 2;"AB" which would otherwise be required. It also makes it easy to call the relevant symbol up when needed in response to the random numbers generated in line 440. Lines 930 and 940 add the parts of the bell and the color yellow together; and 1020 and 1030 do the same for the cherry (actually there are three of them) and magenta.

The letters to enter, where you see the symbols in the printout, are (and these of course are graphics) A and B (line 840); C and D (line 850); E and F (line 930); G and H (line 940); J and K (line 1020); and L and M (line 1030).

The lines from 1040 to 1130 print out the basic fruit machine. The reels will be overprinted on this as the game proceeds.

From the RETURN of that subroutine, we go to the SPIN REELS subroutine starting at line 300. Firstly, $5.00 is subtracted from your money (line 320) to pay for the spin. Next, the variable PRIZE (which will hold your win, if any) is set to zero. Line 350 asks you to press ENTER to "pull the handle" on the fruit machine, and line 360 waits until the keyboard is clear, then moves to 370 to wait for your keypress. Line 380 wipes out the "Press ENTER . . ." instructions. Your money total (now that it is minus $5.00) is printed by line 390, and the routine from 400 to 470 spins the reels eight times, calling up the PRINT REELS subroutine (from line 210) each time it goes through the Z loop.

The B loop, inside the Z loop, generates four numbers at random between one and four, and assigns them to elements one to four of the A array. If you have indicated you wish to hold (which is shown by the value held by that element of the Q array), the program jumps over the random number routine, and goes straight to NEXT B. Line 430 simply creates a pleasant "fruit machine" noise duing the spin. This is *after* the "hold option" check (the element of the array Q) so that there is a different sound if one or more of the reels are held. This will be quite clear when you run the program.

Line 480 sets all elements of the Q array to zero which, in effect, resets the HOLD mechanism to "no holds." Lines 490 to 510 check for the various winning combinations, 490 for a jackpot (four of the same symbol); 500 for a three of a kind, and 510 for two or more bells in a row.

Lines 520 to 540 produce some sounds while you wait for the result of the spin, and your winnings—if any—are added to your MONEY in line 550. Line 570 prints the name of the win (Q$) on the screen, and line 590 prints out the amount of the win (PRIZE) on the body of the fruit machine. If you have scored a bonus (two or three bells in a row), this is indicated by lines 610 and 620. Line 630 produces an interesting *arpeggio* to end the round, line 630 changes the MONEY total and lines 650 to 670 wipe out the win and prize messages. Lines 680 and 690 check to see if you've failed (by going broke) or if you've achieved the object of the game, breaking the bank (by getting more than $500.00). Either of these conditions will end the game.

The PRINT REELS subroutine (from line 210) is fairly straightforward, making use of the elements assigned to the array A$ as was described earlier when I was talking about the user-defined graphics.

The HOLD subroutine, the last we shall consider in the discussion of this program, plays seven clear notes (line 100) then prints up the word HOLD! Here we can see some fairly routine, but useful to note, error-trapping routines. Firstly, the computer expects a string, rather than a numeric input, even though it eventually wants numeric information. This means that a simple touch of ENTER will get the program on its way, whereas the computer cannot accept a "no-number" numeric entry. Line 130 checks to see if the input is, in fact, the null string, and if so sends action to the "unprint" (which you'll understand in a moment) routine, and then to RETURN to get out of the subroutine.

Line 140 takes the first element of the string—Q$(1)—and converts it using VAL into the number equivalent. By taking the first element, we override the possibility that the user may enter more than one number at once. Line 150 assigns this number to the same element number of the array Q—that is, puts Q(1) equal to one, or Q(4) equal to four, as the case may be. Line 170 prints, in a position related to the number entered, HELD and the number, then returns to line 120 for the next input. When the player enters a null string, by pressing ENTER without a preceding number, the computer goes to line 190 which deletes the HELD messages, and then RETURNs to the master loop, at which point line 60 sends the action back to line 30 to begin the loop again.

I suggest you enter this program as it is, for a start, and then work on the various sections. You may wish to add additional symbols and alternative win routines, or—as I suggested at the beginning—a NUDGE facility. Once you understand how this "fruit machine" works, you might like to try and write one which uses 4 symbols, and only three reels, or one which shows the symbols above and below the winning ones (so nine show in a three window version) with some combinations on the diagonals as winners.

GAMBLIN' FEVER

```
  10 REM GAMBLIN' FEVER
  20 REM **************
  30 GO SUB 720: REM VARIABLES
  40 GO SUB 290: REM SPIN REELS
  50 IF RND>.45 THEN GO SUB 70:
REM HOLD
  60 GO TO 40
  70 REM *********************
  80 REM      HOLD
  90 REM *********************
 100 FOR T=1 TO 7: BEEP .1,50-T*
7: NEXT T
 110 PRINT AT 9,22; FLASH 1; INK
RND*4;"HOLD!"
 120 INPUT Q$
 130 IF Q$="" THEN GO TO 190
 140 LET Q=VAL Q$(1)
 150 LET Q(Q)=Q
 170 PRINT AT 9+Q,22; INK RND*4;
FLASH 1;"Held> ";Q;" "
 180 GO TO 120
 190 PRINT AT 9,22;"       ";AT 10
,22;"       ";AT 11,22;"
   ";AT 12,22;"       ";AT 13,22
;"       "
 200 RETURN
 210 REM *********************
 220 REM PRINT REELS
 230 REM *********************
 240 PRINT AT 6,3;A$(A(1));AT 7,
3;B$(A(1))
 250 PRINT AT 6,6;A$(A(2));AT 7,
6;B$(A(2))
 260 PRINT AT 6,9;A$(A(3));AT 7,
9;B$(A(3))
 270 PRINT AT 6,12;A$(A(4));AT 7
,12;B$(A(4))
 280 RETURN
 290 REM *********************
 300 REM   SPIN REELS
 310 REM *********************
 320 LET MONEY=MONEY-5
 330 LET PRIZE=0
 340 LET Q$="": LET P$=""
 350 PRINT AT 4,19; FLASH 1; PAP
ER 1; INK 7;" Press ENTER ";AT 5
,19;" to pull the ";AT 6,21;" ha
ndle "
 360 IF INKEY$<>"" THEN GO TO 36
0
 370 IF INKEY$="" THEN GO TO 370
 380 PRINT AT 4,19;"
";AT 5,19;"             ";AT 6,
21;"      "
 390 PRINT AT 2,28; FLASH 1; INV
ERSE 1; INK RND*4;MONEY; FLASH 0
; INVERSE 0;"  "
 400 FOR Z=1 TO 8
 410 FOR B=1 TO 4
 420 IF Q(B)=B THEN GO TO 450
```

```
 430 BEEP .008,Z*B
 440 LET A(B)=INT (RND*3)+1
 450 NEXT B
 460 GO SUB 210
 470 NEXT Z
 480 DIM Q(4)
 490 IF A(1)=A(2) AND A(2)=A(3)
AND A(3)=A(4) THEN LET Q$=" JACK
POT!! ": LET PRIZE=100: GO TO 52
0
 500 IF (A(1)=A(3) AND A(3)=A(4)
) OR (A(1)=A(2) AND A(2)=A(3)) O
R (A(2)=A(3) AND A(3)=A(4)) OR (
A(2)=A(3) AND A(3)=A(4)) OR (A(1
)=A(2) AND A(2)=A(4)) THEN LET Q
$=" 3 OF A KIND!! ": LET PRIZE=3
5
 510 IF A(1)=2 AND A(2)=2 OR A(2
)=2 AND A(3)=2 OR A(3)=2 AND A(4
)=2 THEN LET P$=" BONUS!! ": LET
 PRIZE=PRIZE+15
 520 FOR G=1 TO 30
 530 BEEP .008,50-G: BEEP .008,5
0
 540 NEXT G
 550 LET MONEY=MONEY+PRIZE
 560 IF Q$="" THEN GO TO 630
 570 PRINT AT 19,6; BRIGHT 1; FL
ASH 1; INK 2; PAPER 4;Q$
 580 PRINT TAB 6; BRIGHT 1; FLAS
H 1; INVERSE 1; INK 2; PAPER 4;Q
$
 590 IF PRIZE>0 THEN PRINT AT 10
,3; BRIGHT 1; INK 2;"You win $";
PRIZE
 600 IF P$="" THEN GO TO 630
 610 PRINT AT 10,20; FLASH 1; IN
K 5; PAPER 3;P$
 620 PRINT AT 11,20; INVERSE 1;
FLASH 1; INK 3;P$
 630 FOR T=1 TO 100: BEEP .008,T
-40: NEXT T
 640 PRINT AT 2,28; FLASH 1; INV
ERSE 1; INK RND*4;MONEY; INVERSE
0
 650 PRINT AT 19,6;"
 ";TAB 6;"                     .."
 660 PRINT AT 10,2; INK 0;"█████████
█████"
 670 PRINT AT 10,20;"           ";
AT 11,20;"
 680 IF MONEY<1 THEN PRINT AT 0,
0; FLASH 1;"That's the end, my f
riend","You are broke": STOP
 690 IF MONEY>499 THEN PRINT AT
0,0; FLASH 1;"You've broken the
bank!!": STOP
 700 RETURN
 720 REM *******************
 730 REM VARIABLES/GRAPHICS
 740 REM *******************
 750 LET MONEY=50
 760 DIM A$(3,4): DIM B$(3,4): D
IM A(4): DIM Q(4)
```

```
 770 FOR Z=0 TO 7
 780 READ A: READ B: READ C: REA
D D
 790 POKE USR "A"+Z,A
 800 POKE USR "B"+Z,B
 810 POKE USR "C"+Z,C
 820 POKE USR "D"+Z,D
 830 NEXT Z
 840 LET A$(1)=CHR$ 16+CHR$ 2+"▞
"+"◢"
 850 LET B$(1)=CHR$ 16+CHR$ 2+"◣
"+"▟"
 860 FOR Z=0 TO 7
 870 READ E: READ F: READ G: REA
D H
 880 POKE USR "E"+Z,E
 890 POKE USR "F"+Z,F
 900 POKE USR "G"+Z,G
 910 POKE USR "H"+Z,H
 920 NEXT Z
 930 LET A$(2)=CHR$ 16+CHR$ 6+"▐
"+"▚ "
 940 LET B$(2)=CHR$ 16+CHR$ 6+"▞
"+"▛ "
 950 FOR Z=0 TO 7
 960 READ J: READ K: READ L: REA
D M
 970 POKE USR "J"+Z,J
 980 POKE USR "K"+Z,K
 990 POKE USR "L"+Z,L
1000 POKE USR "M"+Z,M
1010 NEXT Z
1020 LET A$(3)=CHR$ 16+CHR$ 3+"▟
"+"◢"
1030 LET B$(3)=CHR$ 16+CHR$ 3+"◣
"+"▙ "
1040 PAPER 7: CLS : BORDER 7
1050 PRINT AT 1,3; INK 0;"▐
"
1060 PRINT TAB 2; INK 0;"▐ ▌"; IN
K 4; PAPER 2; FLASH 1;"
"; FLASH 0; PAPER 7; INK 0;"
▌";TAB 21; INK 2; FLASH 1;"Money
$";MONEY
1070 PRINT TAB 2; INK 0;"▐ ▌"; IN
VERSE 1; INK 4; PAPER 2; FLASH 1
;"               "; INVERSE 0; FLASH 0
; PAPER 7; INK 0;"▐   ▌"
1080 FOR Z=1 TO 11
1090 PRINT TAB 2;"▐
"
1100 NEXT Z
1110 PRINT TAB 2;"▐ ▌"; PAPER 6; I
NK 3; FLASH 1;"           "; FLA
SH 0; PAPER 7; INK 0;"▐   ▌"
1120 PRINT TAB 2;"▐ ▌"; PAPER 6; I
NK 3; INVERSE 1; FLASH 1;"
"; FLASH 0; INVERSE 0; PAPE
R 7; INK 0;"▐   ▌"
1130 PRINT TAB 2;"▐
"
1140 RETURN
1150 REM APPLE
1160 DATA 0,8,121,254,0,28,63,25
```

```
4,0,48,63,254,15,32,31,254
1170 DATA 31,240,15,252,51,252,7
,248,52,254,1,224,101,254,0,0
1180 REM BELL
1190 DATA 0,128,7,240,0,128,15,2
48,1,192,15,248,3,224,31,252
1200 DATA 3,224,0,128,3,224,1,19
2,3,224,1,192,3,224,0,0
1210 REM CHERRY
1220 DATA 0,0,1,136,0,2,26,8,56,
12,60,16,124,52,126,208
1230 DATA 127,204,61,224,124,20,
25,240,124,36,1,224,56,72,0,224
1240 STOP
```

And here are some sample printouts, though without color and flashing lights they fail completely to do justice to the effect of running the program on your Timex Sinclair:

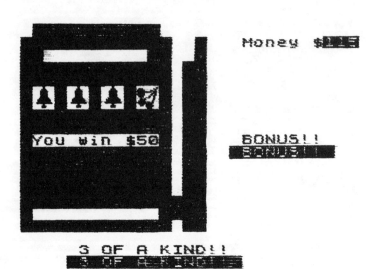

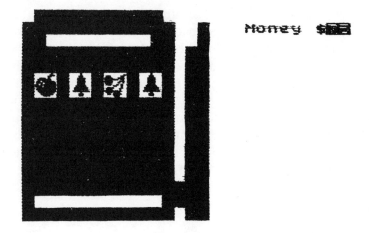

SCREEN$ RACE

I've called this program SCREEN$ RACE because the SCREEN$ function on the Timex Sinclair is the key to the program. The idea of the program is simple. On the screen is a "racetrack," which looks like this:

You start up in the top left hand corner of the screen, as a flashing figure nine. You have to drive this flashing number around the screen in a clockwise direction, using the "R" (up), "F" (left), "J" (right) and "N" (down) keys. You'll find that you'll soon get used to using them for these directions, and they've been chosen because your fingers seem to rest naturally on them (which is more than can be said for the "5," "6," "7" and "8" keys generally used to control on-screen movement).

You have to try and get right around the screen, without bumping into any of the walls. When you get back into the top left hand corner, the nine will change to an eight, and will continue to be reduced by one each time you complete a circuit. Your aim is to get safely around the screen nine times. You are given a rating when you crash which is related to how long you kept your "car" going, and to your score. The score is changed in proportion to how long you have survived that particular round. The score is being decremented all the time you are driving, so it is in your interest to keep the car moving, and not play it too safely. Before you run the program, make sure the CAPS LOCK is on, so that the INKEY$ reading of the keyboard can be interpreted correctly.

SCREEN$ RACE

```
 10 REM  SCREEN$ RACE
 20 REM  ▉ CAPS LOCK ON! ▉
 30 GO SUB 360
 40 FOR Z=9 TO 1 STEP -1
 50 PRINT AT CARD,CARA; BRIGHT
1; FLASH 1;Z
 60 LET SCORE=SCORE-1
 70 LET A1=CARA: LET D1=CARD
 80 IF INKEY$="F" AND CARA>1 TH
EN LET CARA=CARA-1
 90 IF INKEY$="J" AND CARA<30 T
HEN LET CARA=CARA+1
 100 IF INKEY$="R" AND CARD>1 TH
EN LET CARD=CARD-1
 110 IF INKEY$="N" AND CARD<20 T
HEN LET CARD=CARD+1
 120 PRINT AT D1,A1; " "
 130 IF SCREEN$ (CARD,CARA)="X"
THEN GO TO 170
 140 IF CARA<4 AND CARD<4 THEN L
ET CARA=4: LET CARD=1: PRINT AT
D1,A1; " ": BEEP .4,RND*50: NEXT
Z
 150 IF Z=0 THEN GO TO 270
 160 GO TO 50
 170 REM ****CRASH*****
 180 FOR R=1 TO 50: BORDER RND*7
 190 PRINT AT CARD,CARA-1; BRIGH
T 1;"X*X";AT CARD,CARA-1; INVERS
E 1;"*X*"; INVERSE 0
 200 NEXT R: BORDER 2
 210 PRINT AT 3,5; FLASH 1;"Your
 rating is "; INVERSE 1;INT (SCO
RE*3-127*Z)
 220 FOR R=1 TO 50: BEEP .008,R/
50: BEEP .007,50/R: NEXT R
 240 CLS
 250 GO SUB 400
 260 GO TO 40
 270 REM ***SUCCESS***
 280 PRINT AT 5,0; FLASH 1; BRIG
HT 1;"You've done it champ!!"
 290 PRINT INVERSE 1; FLASH 1; B
RIGHT 1; ´TAB 5;" Stand by "
 300 FOR G=1 TO 300: NEXT G
```

```
310 CLS
320 LET SCORE=10000
330 GO SUB 400
340 GO TO 40
350 STOP
360 REM **INITIALISE**
370 PAPER 0: INK 7: CLS
380 BORDER 2
390 LET SCORE=5000
400 PRINT "STARTING SCORE IS ";
FLASH 1;SCORE: PAUSE 300
420 FOR Y=1 TO 0 STEP -1
430 INVERSE Y
440 PRINT AT 0,0;"XXXXXXXXXXXXX
XXXXXXXXXXXXXXXXXXX"
450 PRINT "X                 XX
        XXXXXX"
460 PRINT "X            XX    XX
        XXXX"
470 PRINT "X            XX    XXX
        XX"
480 PRINT "XX           XX    XXX
        XX"
490 PRINT "X            X
        X"
500 PRINT "XX           XXX
XXXX        X"
510 PRINT "XXX          XXXXXX  XX
XXXX        X"
520 PRINT "XXXX         XXXX
 XXXXX       X"
530 PRINT "XXXX         XXXXX     X
XXXXXX      XX"
540 PRINT "XXXX         XXXXX
XXXXXX      XX"
550 PRINT "XXXXXX          XXXXX
   XXX     XX"
560 PRINT "XXXXXX           XXXXX
 XXXXXX      X"
570 PRINT "XXXXXX           XXXXX
 XXXXXX      X"
580 PRINT "XXXXXXX          XXXXXXX
XXXXXXX      X"
590 PRINT "XXXXXXXX         XXXXXX
XXXXX     XXX"
600 PRINT "XXXXXXXXXXX    XXXXXXX
XX       XX"
610 PRINT "XXXXXXXXXX          XXXX
XXX     XXXXX"
620 PRINT "XXXX
        XXXX"
630 PRINT "XXX             XX
   XXXXX"
640 PRINT "XXXX          XXXX
    XXXXXX"
650 PRINT "XXXXXXXXXXXXXXXXXXXXXXX
XXXXXXXXXXXX"
660 NEXT Y
670 LET CARA=4
680 LET CARD=1
690 RETURN
700 REM R IS UP
710 REM F IS LEFT
720 REM J IS RIGHT
730 REM N IS DOWN
740 STOP
```

Action goes to the subroutine starting at 369 when you first run the program. This subroutine, at the end of the program like many of the programs in this book, initializes the variables you'll need. The PAPER color is set to black, the INK to white, and the BORDER to red. The starting score is set to 5000. Line 400 prints the starting score on the screen, and holds it for a few seconds.

The Y loop (lines 420 to 660) prints out the racetrack twice, which gives a most effective start to a round, as you'll see when you run the program. The position of the car across the screen is given by the variable CARA and the position of it down is CARD.

On return from the subroutine to the main program, a loop (Z) is started which counts down from nine to one. The car is printed (line 50) and the score is decremented by one (60). Line 70 sets two new variables (A1 and D1) to the car location, so that the car can be "unprinted" once it has been moved. Lines 80 to 110 read the keyboard, with line 120 "unprinting" the car from its old position. Line 140 checks to see if the car is back within the innermost squares of the top left hand corner of the track, and if it is, sends action back to the next run through the Z loop. Line 150 checks to see if the Z loop is over (which means you've won), and if it finds that it is over, sends action to the SUCCESS routine, starting at line 270. If Z does not equal zero (i.e., the final circuit has not been made), line 160 sends action back—still within the same run of the Z loop—to line 50, where the car is printed in its new position, and the circuit begins again.

Line 130 was left out of this discussion because I wanted to talk about it at more length than some of the others, and because one of the effects of line 130 is to send action to the routine which follows the point we've just been discussing, the CRASH routine starting at 170. Have a look at line 130. It uses the SCREEN$ function to do one of its two tasks on the Timex Sinclair (the other is to save or load back a full screen picture from the television to tape) which is to examine the contents of a specific location. In some of the previous games (such as FIELD OF SKULLS and JACK-MAN), the function has been used for the same purpose.

The two numbers which follow the word SCREEN$ in brackets are the same as the PRINT AT locations of the place on the screen we wish to examine. Line 130 looks at the position CARD, CARA which is where the flashing number "car" will next be printed. If it finds an X there, it knows the car is about to crash, and so directs the program to the CRASH routine starting at line 170. If it does not find an X there, the program continues on through the loop. If you decide to make your track out of characters other than X's (and remember, SCREEN$ will not read graphics characters), make sure you change the X in line 130 to whatever character you make the walls out of.

The CRASH routine is interesting, producing some pyrotechnical effects which you can probably employ in other programs. The R loop (lines 180 to 200) prints a design ("X*X, alternating with "*X*") just where the car has crashed, while changing the BORDER randomly. This random

BORDER change is quite alarming and may even, as it does with my television set, cause the central picture area to bulge slightly, and produce some weird crackling noises from the set. Once we've endured the R loop, the BORDER is reset to red (the second statement in line 200) and then the score is printed up on the screen, as a "rating" (three times the score, minus 127 times the Z you were at when you crashed). Line 220 produces a loop of sound, somewhat like those discussed in Chapter 3, on sound. Line 250 sends action to a line just after the one where the score is set at the very start of the game, so that your new score is not increased.

The SUCCESS routine, from line 270, is only called if you manage to get all nine digits around the screen safely, a really formidable achievement. It can be done, but only after a great deal of practice. "You've done it champ!!" you're told, and your score is changed to 10000. From there the program follows the same route as it does at the end of the CRASH routine.

There are many things you can do to change this program. You may prefer to define a little graphics car and only aim to get it around the track once. You may wish to add sound.

Do not feel constrained to stick with my race track. Try mine out first, and then change or complicate it in any way you like. You may even like to write a routine to generate a new track every round at random, or switch between two or more of them. You'll find that it is quite easy to cheat in this program, by simply driving your car backwards into the area in the top left hand corner, and holding it there while the Z loop is decremented. You may wish to write a routine to stop cheats from doing this.

SPAWN

SPAWN is a variant of the famous John Conway game of LIFE. In this version, a number of little green frogs dance around the screen creating the patterns for which LIFE is famous. The game of LIFE was invented by Mr. Conway, of Cambridge University, in October, 1970. It simulates the birth, death and growth of cells in a closed colony. This, however, is no Malthusian nightmare, in which the cells breed ceaselessly until they run out of food or room. In the world of LIFE, and of its offspring, SPAWN, birth, death and survival follow most civilized rules.

The cells live on a grid, and follow these rules drawn up by Conway:

- There are eight neighbors for each cell on the grid
- Survival to the next generation occurs when a cell has two or three neighbors—no more, and no less
- If there are three surrounding cells, and the place on the grid being checked is empty, then a new cell will be born in that spot on the grid in the next generation
- Any cell with four or more neighbors dies in the following generation

There are a number of ways to write this program, and I suggest you
might like to try and write it yourself before seeing how I have done it with
the spawning frogs. There is, however, one additional piece of information you need to construct the game properly: the rules must be applied all
over the grid at the same time, so that changes for the coming generation
do not effect cells which have not yet been checked in the present generation. Set up a 10 by 10 grid, and try to work out a program to place cells on
it and check those cells in accordance with Conway's rules—which you'll
have to do by working out a routine to "circumnavigate" the grid position
being checked.

Here is my listing, which you may want to use as a starting point for
your own program, or may simply want to run to see what SPAWN looks
like in practice, so you'll know what you're aiming at.

SPAWN

```
10 REM ***************
20 REM        SPAWN
30 REM ***************
40 GO SUB 260
50 BEEP .008,RND*40: BORDER RN
D*7
60 PRINT AT 2,6; INK 2; FLASH
1; BRIGHT 1;" Spawning ";Z;" ";
AT 5,0;
70 FOR M=2 TO 9: PRINT TAB 6;
80 FOR N=2 TO 9
90 LET X(M,N)=Y(M,N)
100 PRINT INK 4;CHR$ (X(M,N));"
";
110 NEXT N
120 PRINT
130 NEXT M
140 FOR M=2 TO 9
150 FOR N=2 TO 9
160 LET Q=0
170 FOR W=1 TO 8
180 LET Q=Q+(VAL A$(W) =144)
190 NEXT W
200 IF X(M,N) =144 AND Q<>2 AND
Q<>3 THEN LET Y(M,N) =32
210 IF X(M,N) =32 AND Q=3 THEN L
ET Y(M,N) =144
220 NEXT N
230 NEXT M
240 LET Z=Z+1
250 GO TO 50
260 REM ** INITIALISATION **
270 RESTORE
280 DIM A$(8,10): DIM X(10,10):
DIM Y(10,10)
290 FOR Q=1 TO 8
300 READ Q$
310 LET A$(Q) =Q$
320 NEXT Q
```

```
 330 DATA "X(M-1,N-1)","X(M-1,N)
","X(M-1,N+1)","X(M,N-1)","X(M,N
+1)","X(M+1,N-1)","X(M+1,N)","X(
M+1,N+1)"
 340 REM INITIAL CULTURE
 350 FOR P=1 TO 10
 360 FOR Q=1 TO 10
 370 LET X(P,Q)=32: LET Y(P,Q)=3
2
 380 NEXT Q
 390 NEXT P
 400 FOR Q=1 TO 15
 410 READ A
 420 READ B
 430 LET X(A,B)=144: LET Y(A,B)=
144
 440 NEXT Q
 450 DATA 3,4,3,5,3,6,4,3,4,5,4,
7,5,4,5,5,5,6,6,3,6,5,6,7,7,4,7,
5,7,6
 460 FOR Q=0 TO 7
 470 READ P
 480 POKE USR "A"+Q,P
 490 NEXT Q
 500 DATA 66,153,90,60,24,126,66
,102
 510 LET Z=1
 520 RETURN
```

I'll go through it to explain what each of the sections of the program is doing. We go first to the subroutine from line 260, where intialization occurs. Line 280 dimensions three arrays: A$ (to hold the mathematical relationships which exist between a grid position and the positions which need to be checked around it); X (to hold the "current generation"); and Y (to hold the "following generation" which is formed while the current generation is on the screen).

The loop from 290 to 320 reads the DATA statement at line 330, and places each of the "position formulas" into successive elements of Q$. Lines 350 to 390 fill the grid up with empty spaces (32 is the Timex Sinclair code for an empty space), and also fills the "following generation" with empty spaces. Lines 400 and 440 read the first generation information, held in DATA statement 450, into both grids. The number they are assigning to the array elements is 144, the character code of the first user-defined graphic (graphic A).

The final Q loop, from 460 to 490, defines the shape of the frog that will be printed as CHR$ 144 in due course. Z, the number of the spawning, is set to 1, for the first generation.

On our return from the initialization subroutine, there is a BEEP, and the BORDER flashes. The number of the spawning is printed at the top of the screen, and the loop from 70 to 130 prints out the colony. Line 90 first reads the "following generation" information (the Y array) into the "current generation" (X array). It is the X array which is printed.

The next loop, from 140 to 230, is the most important one for the working of the program. Q, set to zero in line 160, is the variable assigned to count the cells surrounding the one under consideration. The W loop, lines 170 to 190, is the magic one which checks the eight cells surrounding any cell under consideration. Notice that M and N, the two master controls of the checking loop, only move from 2 to 9, so that cells on the extreme outside (which do not have eight neighbors) are not checked. Line 180 increments the value of Q by one each time the expression VAL A\$(W)=144 is found to be true. The Timex Sinclair assigns a value of one to a true statement, so this line is a slightly shortened way of saying: IF VAL A\$(W) = 144 THEN LET Q = Q + 1.

Once the neighbors have been checked, the program acts on the count. If the cell under consideration contains a frog (i.e., contains the value 144) and there are not two or three neighbors (i.e., Q is not equal to two and is not equal to three) then the corresponding cell for the next generation (held, you'll recall in the Y array) is set to 32. If, however, the cell being checked is empty (contains the value 32) and there are three neighbors (Q equals three) then the next generation element is set to 144, and a birth occurs.

Once this process has been repeated for the whole grid (except for the cells on the outside of the grid), the spawning count is incremented by one (line 240) and the program returns to line 50 to print out the new generation, and start the process again.

You can add your own starting colonies to this program by changing the DATA statement, line 450, where the numbers are in pairs, relating to the A and B within the X and Y elements in line 430. One pattern which you might like to try, once you've run the one contained in the original program, is:

```
450 DATA 3,3,3,5,3,6,3,8,6,3,6,
8,9,5,9,6,4,4,4,7,5,4,5,7,6,5,6,
6,7,5,7,6,8,3,8,4,8,7,8,8,9,3,9,
4,9,7,9,8
```

Note that there are 24 elements in the original spawning, so you'll have to change the 15 at the end of line 400 into a 24. This pattern lasts for 16 generations before dying out. Once you've seen it go through the very attractive patterns it forms in these 16 generations, add a single cell to the original colony, or delete one, and see how this single change effects every generation from then on.

You may wish to write a routine to set up the initial colony at random, or one which allows you to enter the starting colony at the beginning of each run, in response to computer prompts. When you're working out the initial colonies, set up a 10 by 10 grid, and number the squares one to ten along the top and from one to ten down the side, and then read off their numbers. Do not place any starting cells in the outermost "frame" of the grid.

Finally, here are a few patterns of dancing frogs, from SPAWN:

Spawning   1

Spawning   2

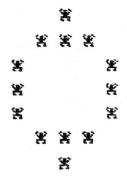

Spawning   3

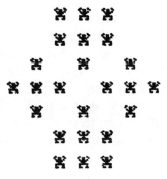

Spawning   4

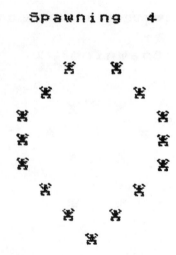

WORKIN' FOR THE MAN—A SIMULATION

In WORKIN' FOR THE MAN, you are The Man, the boss of a factory producing Zibbies. You have almost total control of your staff, their output and your selling price. Your task is to stay in business for as long as possible, and perhaps to make a million.

This program is a simulation, a program in which the computer takes the role of "reality," manipulating information to some extent as it would be manipulated in real life.

The two key words in creating a simulation are "replication" and "simplification." We attempt to replicate life, but because there is no way of including every conceivable factor we simplify to some extent to end up with a manageable set of variables to work with.

In this program, which explains itself as it runs, you are, as we've said, in charge of a Zibbie factory. At the start of the run, you are told how many people you have on your staff, how much they are paid each week, how much capital you have on hand, how much stock in your store room, and the selling price of Zibbies. The program tells you your total wage bill, and this is the one figure you must always keep in mind. The program works in weeks, and you must manage to meet your wage and raw material commitments each week, or you will go bankrupt.

The first choice you are offered in a round is that of hiring or firing staff. While your employees' union is quite happy for you to hire staff, there is some resistance to firing, so despite your best intentions, you are only allowed to get rid of the number of staff they suggest. You may enter "7" when you are asked how many you wish to fire, and the computer may well reply "Unions allow you to fire 2" which means, as in real life, you do not have total, immediate control over the size of your staff. And as each staff member can only make a certain number of Zibbies each week, you cannot keep your factory alive just by cutting the staff to one.

From time to time, the workers will demand a pay raise, and you have no choice but to pay it. Your suppliers, as well, are well known for making intemperate price increases in raw materials, so you are waging a perpetual war against rising prices and wages.

You have three factors you can control, within limits:

1. The number of people on your staff (you cannot fire with impunity; each staff member, of course, costs money each week to keep; and the maximum output per person is limited).
2. The number of Zibbies you will make each week (you set the production target, which is rarely, if ever, completely met).
3. The selling price, which can be changed at your whim (but each change makes it harder to sell your stock in hand; you do not sell every Zibbie in hand every week, and the number you do sell is related, in part, to you keeping your prices unchanged).

As you pay your bills, you have to increase your prices from time to time (because the payroll is increasing, and so is the bill from your raw materials supplier) but the knowledge that each change in the price decreases the selling power of your product should moderate your price changes.

This description may sound a little bewildering, but don't worry. You don't have to remember all this, as the program does most of the work, and explains it to you as the game unfolds.

WORKIN' FOR THE MAN can end in one of two ways. The most usual is bankruptcy, when you'll be told how many weeks you managed to keep the factory going. The second way the program can end is if you manage to build up a million dollars (capital plus stock in hand). As you'll discover when you play this game, the cards are stacked against you. It is a saying in business life that the first job a business must do is ensure its own survival. You'll discover how true this is when you try to run your Zibbie factory. And despite the great simplification which has occurred to make this a manageable simulation, it replicates reality in quite an uncanny way. You'll find yourself actually despairing when some sales or production figures come in, and will agonize over your hiring/firing and price-setting decisions.

Despite its awesome length, WORKIN' FOR THE MAN is actually a relatively simple program, and once you understand its layout you'll find it relatively easy to create simulations of your own from scratch.

As we've suggested several times in the book, you can often make mammoth programming tasks far more manageable if you start the job by creating a small number of subroutine calls which rotate within a master loop at the beginning of a program. This is the way WORKIN' FOR THE MAN was written. Here, first of all, is the program listing. A discussion of it will follow.

WORKIN' FOR THE MAN

```
  10 REM  ***********************
  20 REM  WORKIN' FOR THE MAN
  30 REM  ***********************
  40 GO SUB 9000: REM VARIABLES
  50 LET WEEK=WEEK+1
 100 GO SUB 5000: REM PRINTOUT
 110 GO SUB 6000: REM PEOPLE
 120 GO SUB 5000: REM PRINTOUT
 130 GO SUB 5130: REM MAKE
 140 GO SUB 5000: REM PRINTOUT
 150 GO SUB 4000: REM SALES
 160 GO SUB 3000: REM
            UNPREDICTABLES
 170 LET CAPITAL=CAPITAL-WAGE*WO
RKFORCE
 180 GO TO 50
2990 REM  *********************
3000 REM UNPREDICTABLES
3005 CLS
3010 IF RND<.45 THEN GO TO 3100
3020 LET A=INT (RND*7)+1
3025 BEEP .5,RND*50: BEEP .4,RND
*50
3030 PRINT ''"Unions demand ";A;
"% payrise"
3040 LET WAGE=INT (100*(WAGE+(A*
WAGE/100)))/100
3050 PAUSE 100
3060 PRINT '''"Pay per employee
is now $";WAGE
3070 PAUSE 100
3075 BEEP .5,RND*50: BEEP .4,RND
*50
3080 CLS
3100 IF RND<.85 THEN GO TO 3190
3110 PRINT '' INK 2; FLASH 1;"F
lash flood ruins some of your","
stock",,,,"Stand by for damage r
eport:",
3120 PAUSE 100
3130 LET A=INT (RND*STOCK/2)+1
3140 LET STOCK=STOCK-A
3150 PRINT '' INK 1; FLASH 1;"To
tal stock destroyed was",A;" Zib
bies, worth $";A*SELLPRICE;" ret
ail"
3160 PAUSE 100
3170 PRINT '''"Stock on hand is n
ow ";STOCK
3180 PAUSE 100
3190 IF RND>.3 THEN GO TO 3290
3195 CLS
3200 PRINT ''"Supplier announces
 dramatic","price rise!"
3210 PAUSE 100
3220 LET A=INT ((RND*100*COST/7)
)/100
3225 IF A<.01 THEN GO TO 3220
3230 PRINT '''"Cost of making Zib
bies","goes up by "; FLASH 1; IN
K 2;"$";A; FLASH 0; INK 0;" each
"
```

```
3240 PAUSE 100
3250 LET COST=COST+A
3260 PRINT ''  INK 7; PAPER 1;" I
t now costs "; FLASH 1; INK 7; P
APER 0;"$";COST;" "
3270 PRINT "to make each one"
3280 PAUSE 100
3290 IF RND<.65 AND MAKE<SELLPRI
CE THEN RETURN
3300 CLS
3305 BEEP .5,RND*50: BEEP .4,RND
*50
3310 PRINT ''"You have a chance
to raise","your price"
3320 PRINT ''"Zibbies now sell fo
r $";SELLPRICE
3330 PAUSE 100
3340 INPUT FLASH 1;"What percent
age increase? ";A
3345 IF A>0 THEN LET Z=Z+A
3350 LET SELLPRICE=INT (100*(SEL
LPRICE+A*SELLPRICE/100))/100
3360 PAUSE 50
3370 PRINT ' FLASH 1; INK 3;"Zib
bies now sell for $";SELLPRICE
3380 PAUSE 100
3390 RETURN
3990 REM *************************
4000 REM SALES
4005 BEEP .5,RND*50: BEEP .4,RND
*50
4010 PRINT FLASH 1; PAPER 5;'"To
tal stock is ";STOCK
4015 PAUSE 100
4020 PRINT FLASH 1; PAPER 3;'"St
and by for sales report....."
4025 PAUSE 300
4030 CLS
4040 LET A=INT (RND*STOCK/(Z/100
))+1
4045 PAPER RND*6: CLS : BORDER R
ND*6
4050 IF A>STOCK THEN GO TO 4040
4055 BORDER 7: PAPER 7: CLS
4060 PRINT '' INK 1;"Total Zibbi
es sold: ";A
4070 LET STOCK=STOCK-A
4080 PRINT '"Income from sale: $
";A*SELLPRICE
4090 LET CAPITAL=CAPITAL+A*SELLP
RICE
4095 PAUSE 100
4100 RETURN
5000 REM ***********************
5010 REM    PRINT OUT
5020 FOR G=40 TO 50: BEEP .008,G
: BEEP .008,60-2*G: NEXT G
5022 CLS
5025 IF CAPITAL+STOCK<1 THEN GO
TO 8000: REM BANKRUPT
5027 IF CAPITAL+STOCK>999999 THE
N PRINT FLASH 1; BRIGHT 1; INK 2
;"You've made a million!!": PAUS
E 500: GO TO 8050
```

```
5030 PRINT INK 2; FLASH 1;".  FAC
TORY REPORT: WEEK ";WEEK;"  "
5040 PRINT ' INK 2;"Capital on h
and is $";CAPITAL
5050 PRINT ' INK 1;"Your stores
hold ";STOCK;" Zibbies";TAB 10;"
worth $";STOCK*SELLPRICE
5060 PRINT INK 2;'"They sell for
 $";SELLPRICE;" each"
5070 PRINT INK 2;"and cost $";CO
ST;" each to make"
5080 PRINT INK 7; PAPER 1;'"Work
force is ";WORKFORCE;" people"
5090 PRINT PAPER 1; INK 7;"Their
 wages are $";WAGE;" each","  and
 the wage bill this week"," is $
";WAGE*WORKFORCE
5100 PRINT INK 2;'"Each person c
an make ";PRODUCE;" Zibbies a we
ek, a total output of ";PRODUCE*
WORKFORCE
5120 RETURN
5130 INPUT "How many do you want
 to make? ";MAKE
5135 IF MAKE=0 THEN RETURN
5140 IF MAKE*COST>CAPITAL THEN P
RINT INK 2; FLASH 1;"Not enough
money": GO TO 5130
5150 IF MAKE>PRODUCE*WORKFORCE T
HEN PRINT INK 4; FLASH 1;"Not en
ough people": GO TO 5130
5160 PRINT AT 0,0; FLASH 1; INK
1;"    Target week ";WEEK;" is "
;MAKE;"  "
5170 LET MAKE=MAKE-INT (RND*MAKE
/5*(Z/100))
5180 PAUSE 100
5190 PRINT INK 3; FLASH 1;AT 0,0
;"Total made in week ";WEEK;" wa
s ";MAKE;"  "
5200 LET STOCK=STOCK+MAKE
5210 LET CAPITAL=CAPITAL-COST*MA
KE
5220 PAUSE 50
5300 RETURN
5310 REM **********************
6000 REM ***PEOPLE***
6010 INPUT "How many people do y
ou want","to hire? ";A
6020 LET WORKFORCE=WORKFORCE+A
6030 PRINT AT 0,0; FLASH 1; INK
1;"    Total workforce is ";WORK
FORCE
6035 PAUSE 100: GO SUB 5000
6037 IF A>0 THEN RETURN
6040 INPUT "How many people do y
ou want","to "; FLASH 1; INK 4;"
fire? ";A
6042 IF A=0 THEN GO TO 6090
6045 IF A>WORKFORCE THEN GO TO 6
040
6050 LET A=INT (RND*A+1)
6060 PAUSE 100
6070 PRINT FLASH 1; BRIGHT 1; IN
```

```
K 6; PAPER 2;'''"Unions allow yo
u to fire ";A
6080 LET WORKFORCE=WORKFORCE-A
6090 PAUSE 100
6100 RETURN
7990 REM ********************
8000 REM BANKRUPTCY
8010 PRINT '''TAB 8; FLASH 1; IN
K 2;"BANKRUPT!!!!"
8020 PRINT '''"Oh the shame of i
t!"
8030 PRINT '''"Still, you kept t
he business"
8040 PRINT "going for "; FLASH 1
; INK 1;WEEK; FLASH 0; INK 0;" w
eeks"
8050 PRINT '''"Enter "Y" for anot
her try, or","N" to give up"
8055 LET A$=INKEY$
8060 IF A$="" THEN GO TO 8055
8070 IF A$="Y" OR A$="y" THEN RU
N
8080 STOP
9000 REM *********************
9010 REM VARIABLES
9020 REM *********************
9030 LET CAPITAL=500+INT (RND*50
0)
9040 LET STOCK=100+INT (RND*50)
9050 LET SELLPRICE=10+INT (RND*5
)
9060 LET COST=2+INT (RND*5)
9070 IF COST>SELLPRICE THEN GO T
O 9050
9080 LET WORKFORCE=7+INT (RND*10
)
9090 LET WAGE=12+INT (RND*SELLPR
ICE*5)
9100 LET PRODUCE=5+INT (RND*6)
9110 LET WEEK=0
9120 REM Z is sales resistance
              factor
9130 LET Z=1
9140 PAPER 7: CLS : BORDER 7: IN
K 0
9500 RETURN
```

We start with the loop from 40 to 180:

- GOSUB 9000—This sets up the variables (which change from game to game) which determine such things as the number of people on your staff, their initial wages, the stock in hand, the selling price of Zibbies and so on.
- Line 50 increments the variable WEEK by one.
- The subroutine starting at 5000 is called several times throughout the loop (by lines 100, 120, 140) to show the changing status during the week.
- The other subroutines do what the following REM statements indicate: PEOPLE (hire/fire, from 6000); MAKE (production, from 5130) and SALES (from 4000)

- The final subroutine (UNPREDICTABLES, from 3000) is traversed each "week" of the factory's life, but the elements in it may be bypassed, either completely or in part. The UNPREDICTABLES (which include union demands for more money and flash floods which destroy part of your stock in hand) are designed to keep the going tough, but are not so arbitrary as to destroy the importance of skill in maintaining the health of your factory

To write a simulation, you first need to work out in your own mind what is being replicated, and which variables you will emulate in the program. Once you've done this, you need to set up the starting loop to control the program. My next step, and one which you may want to follow, is to create the standard printout (in this case, from line 5000) even before you do such things as assign variables. You'll discover that setting up the standard printout will tell you each variable you need. In this program, as in others in the book, I've used explicit names for variables, so you do not need to maintain a separate register to tell you, for example, that ZA3 is the wages and BB is the stock in the warehouse. This sort of random variable naming can lead to great confusion. Although it takes a little longer to type in long, explicit names, the trouble it will save you is well worth the time it takes.

As the printout was the key to writing this program, it makes sense to look at it first. Here is part of a printout:

```
FACTORY REPORT: WEEK 5

Capital on hand is $2657.92

Your stores hold 12 Zibbies
          worth $169.68

They sell for $14.14 each
and cost $7.41 each to make

Workforce is 7 people
Their wages are $41 each
 and the wage bill this week
 is $287

Each person can make 10 Zibbies
a week, a total output of 70
```

The printout tells you which week it is, how much capital you have (from which you must pay wages and buy raw materials), the number of Zibbies you have in stock, the selling prices and cost of production, the number of people on your staff, their individual wages and the total for the workforce, and—finally—the number of Zibbies they can each make per week, assuming they all work at 100% efficiency (which they rarely do, as you'll discover).

This printout or a variation of it appears throughout the game, using color and flashing to highlight the different elements in it, making it easier to read. When you first run the program you'll see the starting parameters that fate has decreed for you, and then the program will go to the PEOPLE subroutine, starting at line 6000. "How many people do you want to hire?" you are asked. If you decide to hire any, they are added to the workforce, the standard printout re-appears with the total payroll recalculated and you continue with the next section of your task, determining how many Zibbies you will make.

If, however, you decide not to hire any more people, you will be asked "How many people do you want to fire?" This is the point where the union becomes troublesome, and dictates just how many people they will let you get rid of. Again the standard printout will reappear, with the new workforce total and payroll displayed.

Having survived the staff situation, you then face production decisions (with the subroutine starting at line 5130—MAKE). "How many do you want to make?" you are asked. If you enter zero, the program returns to the main printout, and goes into the SALES routine, to sell from your stock. If, however, you decide you want to try and make some Zibbies, the program will compare your production target with (a) the number of people you have working for you that week, keeping in mind that each person has a limited output; and with (b) the cost of the material used in each one. If you do not have enough people, you'll be told (NOT ENOUGH PEOPLE is the message) and be asked to enter another production target. In a similar way, NOT ENOUGH MONEY will come up on the screen if you set a target which will demand more raw materials than you can afford. Once you get a target the simulation will accept, it will print on the screen at the top "Target week 4 is 92" or whatever. After a short pause, the message "Total made in week 4 was 86" or however many were made that week will appear.

Too explicit a series of instructions will diminish the pleasure you may have running this simulation, so I will stop at this point. After all, I want to leave you a few surprises when you get it underway. And by now, if you've followed through the explanations given for the other games, you should be able to work your way through this program without too much trouble.

This program has been included in this book because simulations are one of the very useful areas in which computers can serve us. Creating your own simulations, from running a space station to a pancake-making works, can be a good indication as to how simulations are created in real life, and how difficult it is to create computer models of real life situations. For example, a real Zibbie factory would have to allow for contingencies such as the possibility of workers being injured on the job or not turning up because they are sick, or working slowly because it is hot, someone's birthday, Friday, close to Christmas, or whatever.

There could be delays in getting supplies to the factory, or vital machinery might break. There could be a fire, an electrical blackout, a union lockout . . . and so on. You'll soon learn the difficulties of trying to too closely replicate the reality reflected in your simulation.

That brings us to the end of the games section in the book. It has been the largest one in the book because I believe that game playing and writing is the surest (and least unpleasant) way to develop programming skills. Games also provide some relief from "serious" computer use. I hope the material in this chapter helps with both those aims. Finally, here are some books which you may find of interest.

Suggestions for Further Reading

Ahl, David ed. *BASIC Computer Games.* Newark, N.J.: Creative Computing Press, 1980.

Chisman, Margaret. *"Producing Computer Poetry."* in *The Best of Creative Computing,* Vol 2, edited by David Ahl. Newark, N.J.: Creative Computing Press. Originally appeared as article in *Creative Computing.*

Mateosian, Richard. *Inside BASIC Games.* Berkeley: SYBEX Inc., 1981.

Spencer, Donald D. *Game Playing with BASIC.* Rochelle Park, N.J.: Hayden Book Company, Inc., 1981.

Watson, William Scot. *67 Ready-To-Run Programs in BASIC.* Blue Ridge Summit, Pa.: TAB Books, Inc. 1981.

What To Do After You Hit RETURN. Rochelle Park, N.J.: Hayden Book Company, Inc. 1981.

7

Three-dimensional Graphics

Science fiction films like *Star Wars* show computers producing complex three-dimensional images and manipulating them in real time. While this Timex Sinclair program cannot produce images of such complexity, it does manage to produce 3-D images of a sort, and allows you to handle them (by rotation) as if they were real objects.

The program allows you to draw figures using straight lines of a length you choose. The explanation of how to use the program may seem a little bewildering, but if you enter the program before you begin, then follow through the explanation carefully, you should find you gain some real control over the program, and can use it to produce worthwhile 3-D images.

First of all, then, enter this program, then return to the book for an explanation of how to use it.

THREEDEE ETCH

```
1 REM *********************
2 REM     THREEDEE ETCH
3 REM
4 REM *********************
5 DIM S$(255)
6
10 GO SUB 5000
11 GO SUB 1000
```

```
  15 CLS
  20 GO SUB 7000
  35 IF P=1 THEN GO TO 200
  36
  40 LET R$=INKEY$: IF R$="" THE
N GO TO 40
  41 LET S$(A)=R$
  42 LET A=A+1
  43 IF A=255 THEN PRINT "BUFFER
FULL": STOP
  44 IF R$="E" THEN GO TO 10
  50 GO SUB 3000
  60 GO SUB 2000
  70 DRAW C-PEEK (23677),D-PEEK
(23678)
  80 GO TO 40
  90
 200 GO SUB 6000
 205 LET R$=INKEY$: IF R$="" THE
N GO TO 205
 210 GO TO 10
 220
1000 LET S=L*L+M*M
1010 LET T=S+N*N
1020 LET Q=SQR (T)
1030 LET H=SQR (S)
1040 RETURN
2000 LET O=T-U*L-V*M-W*N
2010 LET C=T*(V*L-U*M)*4/(H*Q)+1
28
2020 LET D=96+3*Q*(W*S-N*(U*L+V*
M))/(H*Q)
2286 RETURN
2287
3000 IF R$="U" THEN LET W=W+G
3010 IF R$="D" THEN LET W=W-G
3020 IF R$="R" THEN LET U=U-G
3030 IF R$="L" THEN LET U=U+G
3040 IF R$="B" THEN LET V=V-G
3050 IF R$="F" THEN LET V=V+G
3060 RETURN
3999
5000 CLS
5010 INPUT "SIZE?";G
5020 INPUT "X VIEWPOINT?";L
5030 INPUT "Y VIEWPOINT?";M
5040 INPUT "Z VIEWPOINT?";N
5050 LET A=1
5061 PRINT "'G'-GET"'"'P'-PUT"'"
'R'-RANDOM"
5070 LET R$=INKEY$: IF R$="" THE
N GO TO 5070
5080 IF R$="G" THEN LET P=1: GO
TO 5110
5090 IF R$="P" THEN LET P=0: GO
TO 5110
5093 IF R$="R" THEN GO TO 8000
5100 GO TO 5070
5110 RETURN
5999
6000 GO SUB 7000
6010 LET R$=S$(A)
```

```
6020 GO SUB 3000
6030 GO SUB 2000
6040 DRAW C-PEEK  (22577),D-PEEK
 (23578)
6050 LET A=A+1
6060 IF S$(A)<>"E" AND A<>255 TH
EN GO TO 6010
6070 RETURN
6999
7000 LET W=0: LET U=0: LET V=0:
GO SUB 2000
7010 PLOT C,D
7020 RETURN
7999
8000 LET A=1: LET G=20: LET L=RN
D*100: LET M=RND*100: LET N=RND*
100
8003 CLS
8010 GO SUB 6000
8020 PAUSE 50
8030 GO TO 8000
```

Make sure the computer is in the CAPS LOCK mode (hold down the CAPS SHIFT key, and press the 2 key) before you run this program. When you RUN it, the first thing you will see is the prompt SIZE? at the bottom of the screen. This prompt wants you to enter the size of the lines that go to make up the figures you draw with the program. To give you an idea of the scale the program is using, the lines in the cube in figure one are of length 20. This is a good starting point, so enter 20, then press ENTER.

The next prompt you'll see is X VIEWPOINT?. For this first run, enter 100 for this, and 150 and 20 respectively for the Y and Z viewpoints.

The screen should clear to show you the following:

```
'G'   -GET
'P'   -PUT
'R'   -RANDOM
```

These are the three options which are being offered to you. We'll start by using the PUT option, which you indicate by pressing the "P" key. If nothing happens when you do this, you probably have not engaged CAPS LOCK.

The screen will clear again, leaving a tiny dot in the center. This dot is the starting point of the figure you are to draw.

The program will now accept six different inputs: U(p), D(own), L(eft), R(ight), F(orward), or B(ackward). You just press the initial letter of the direction in order to move. Don't linger too long on any key, or you may end up drawing a line longer than you intended. Play around with the program for a while, pressing the direction keys at random, then return to the book.

Now try this sample drawing:

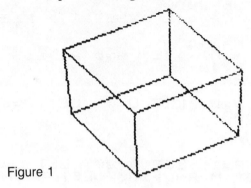

Figure 1

First return to a blank screen, either by typing "E" (for "END") as a direction to be moved in, or start again with RUN. Either method will get you back to the SIZE? prompt. Then use the same figures as I gave before, to get to GET/PUT/RANDOM display. Enter "P", and we're ready to go.

Type "U". This will draw a line from the dot to about three-quarters of the way up the screen. Type "L". This will join a line going to the left to the top of the previous line. Then go down, by pressing "D". You should now have something looking a bit like a gravestone on the screen. We can now join the two ends to make a square by going "R"ight. Now, move forward, with "F", and carry out the above procedure again. You should now see that we only need to add three more lines and we will have a three-dimensional cube, as in figure 1.

To reach the points where the extra lines are to be drawn, we will have to draw over some of the lines already on the screen.

The keypresses required are:

       U, B, F, L, B, F, D, B, F and R.

If you watch the screen closely as you enter these, you should have a good idea of how the Timex Sinclair is following your instructions. It may be worth your while pressing "E" at this point and running through the whole procedure a few more times until you can draw a cube without any mistakes.

Now, to continue our investigation of 3-D graphics, use "E" to return to the SIZE? prompt, and answer as follows:

```
SIZE? 10
X VIEWPOINT? 100
Y VIEWPOINT? 150
Z VIEWPOINT? 200
```

Then choose the GET option from the last menu.

You will find that your cube has been drawn automatically, at a reduced size. If it has not been drawn, you must have used "RUN" to get to the "size" menu, and not the "E" option. The program remembers the keypresses you made in the last shape you drew, and if you run the program from scratch, as far as the Timex Sinclair is concerned there is no previous drawing. You may like to try using "E" and the "GET" option to redraw the cube several times, giving different numbers in reply to the viewpoint prompts.

How does it work? The program always draws your object starting from the coordinates 0,0,0 in three-dimensional space. Your answer to the VIEWPOINT prompt tells the computer from where in space you want the image drawn. The menu (GET/PUT/RANDOM) is asking whether the shape drawn should be constructed from keypresses from the keyboard ("P") or keypresses stored in the program from the last picture ("G"). The "R" option starts an endless sequence of drawing the object from random coordinates and after pausing, drawing it from different co-ordinates. Obviously the "R" option, like the "G" option, requires that there already be an image in memory.

Figure 2 shows a drawing which you may like to try and duplicate.

Figures 3 to 6 show another, rather simpler, image drawn from a number of different viewpoints. Figure 3 is the original figure. Figure 4 is the figure drawn with a smaller "SIZE." Figure 5 is the figure drawn from one end and figure 6 is the figure drawn from underneath. Because the program only produces "wire frame" images it is a little difficult to decide whether figure 6 is from underneath or on top. You will find that complex figures are best drawn with a small step size, such as 10, to allow you to get more detail into the picture.

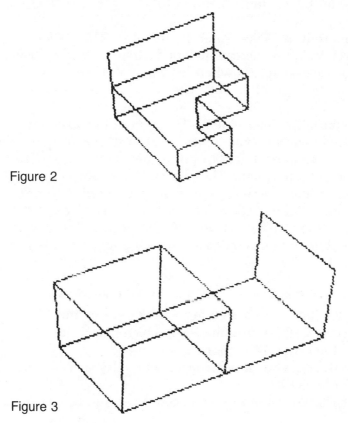

Figure 2

Figure 3

Figure 4   Figure 5   Figure 6

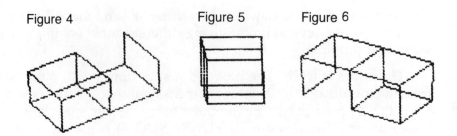

The program is made up of a number of subroutines, which will be covered first. Then I'll go on to talk about the section of code from lines 1 to 210.

Subroutine 1000—New viewpoint. This subroutine takes the new viewpoint, in L, M and N, and using these figures, sets the variables S, T, Q and H. These variables are required later by the plotting algorithm.

Subroutine 2000—Evaluate two-dimensional coordinates. This subroutine returns, in C and D, the screen coordinates corresponding to the point U, V, W. It uses L, M and N, and all the constants defined in subroutine 1000. The constants 128 and 96 in lines 2010 and 2020 are to centralize the image, to ensure the point 0,0,0 is in the center of the screen.

Subroutine 3000—Alter coordinates. The current coordinates U, V, W are incremented or decremented by a set amount (G) for each keypress when the directon keys are used. This subroutine carries this out, with the keypress in R$.

Subroutine 5000—Menu. This subroutine carries out all the initial dialogue with you. Lines 5010 to 5040 ask the now familiar starting questions, line 5061 prints the menu and line 5070 gets the choice for the menu. The variable A in line 5060 is the pointer into the string where all keypresses are stored for the "G" and "R" options. Lines 5080 to 5093 decode the keypress. If "G" was selected, then P is set to true, if "P" is selected, P is set to false. If the random option is called for, then the subroutine at line 8000 is called.

Subroutine 6000—Auto draw. This subroutine automatically draws the figure stored in S$. It is used by the "G" option.
Line 6000: Calls subroutine 7000, which places the initial black dot in the center of the screen.
Line 6010: Gets the next character of S$ in R$ ready for the call to 3000 in line 6020.
Line 6030: Works out the new coordinates to be drawn.

Line 6040: Does an "absolute" DRAW to these new coordinates. The two PEEKs hold the current X and Y coordinates of the Timex Sinclair, and so if these are subtracted from the absolute coordinates to be moved to, an absolute, rather than relative draw is achieved. This technique can be applied to any program where the normal form of the DRAW statement is inappropriate.

Line 6050: Increments the pointer in S$, so that the next character can be examined.

Line 6060: If the character is an "E", indicating the end of the drawing, then RETURNs. Also RETURNs if the string S$ is going to be exceeded when the next line is drawn.

Line 6070: Loops back for the rest of the characters in S$.

Subroutine 7000—Moves the current coordinates to 0,0,0 and plots a point there.

Subroutine 8000—Sets A, G (the size), L, M and N, then draws the figure (line 8010), PAUSEs, then goes back and draws it again from different coordinates.

Line 5: Dimensions S$.

Line 10: Calls subroutine 5000.

Line 11: Calls subroutine 1000.

Line 15: Clears the screen.

Line 20: Calls subroutine 7000.

Line 35: Goes to line 200 if the "G" option was used.

Line 40: Gets a direction keypress.

Line 41: Stores the keypress in S$.

Line 42: Increments the pointer A.

Line 43: Stops the program if S$ has been executed, i.e., if more than 255 keypresses were made.

Line 44: Returns to the starting menu if "E" was pressed.

Line 50: Acts on the keypresses,

Line 60: decodes the coordinates and

Line 70: draws to the new position (see description for line 6040):

Line 80: Loops back for more keypresses.

Line 200: Calls subroutine 6000 for GET option, then, at line 205, waits for a keypress, then loops back at line 210 for the main menu.

8
■

Introduction to Machine Code

You may recall at the very start of the book we spoke of computer languages in "levels," with high level languages, like BASIC, being fairly close to English, and lower level ones being closer to the actual language the microprocessor, the thinking part of your computer, uses. The language used by the microprocessor (the Z80 in a Timex Sinclair) is the language we call machine code. If you talk to your Timex Sinclair in BASIC, part of the computer has spent time translating the BASIC message into machine code, so the microprocessor can understand it. Now this translation can take some time, which is why BASIC is a fairly slow language. As we'll demonstrate now, machine code is very much faster.

Type in and run this program:

```
10   CLEAR32000
20   RESTORE
30   FORa=0 TO 15: READ x: POKE 32000 + a, x:NEXT a
40   DATA33,255,63,01,01,24,22,255,35,11,120,177,
     200,114,24,248
50   CLS: PAUSE 20: RANDOMIZE USR 32000:
     PAUSE 20: GO TO 50
```

This demonstrates how quickly the screen can be filled. Now compare it with the BASIC equivalent:

```
10   FOR a=1 TO 704: PRINT "*";: NEXT a
```

NOTE: It is not fair to judge the lengths of these two programs as, for the main part, the first program is far longer than necessary (we will see why later).

The computer itself only understands long streams of digits. For example, one instruction for the Z80 is 00111101, which means absolutely nothing to most of us. (Note that the Z80 accepts eight-digit codes, which means that the maximum number it can handle is 11111111 or 255 in base 10, the number system we use in everyday life). This "stream" of ones and zeros is a binary number. A number in our normal system, base 10, has digits between 0 and 9, and a binary number, a number in base 2 has digits between 0 and 1. If we look at a number in base 10, the right-most digit is the units, the next digit is 1's (or ten to the power 1), the next being 100's (or ten to the power of 2), and so on. For example: 101 is equal to 1 unit, 0×10 and 1×100.

Base 2 works on the same principle. The first digit on the right is again the units (2 to the power of 0), the next digit being 2's (2 to the power of 1) and the next digit being 4's (2 to the power of 2). For example, in binary: 101 is equal to 1 unit, 0×2 and 1×4 which is 5 in base 10. So if we take 11111111, which is the highest number that the Z80 can handle it looks like this:

```
     1 times 1
   +1 times 2
   +1 times 4
   +1 times 8
   +1 times 16
   +1 times 32
   +1 times 64
   +1 times 128
   = 255
```

While we are on the subject of binary numbers, it would be useful to clear up one topic which can cause a lot of problems. When talking about computers we often hear the terms "bit" and "byte." A bit is one of the digits of the binary number. For example, in the number 00111010, there are eight bits. We can talk about parts of a binary number by referring to the bits which make it up. Bit 0 (the right-most digit) is, in our example, 0, and bit 3 (the fourth digit from the right) is 1. Byte is the term for a number which has 8 bits, so 10101101 is a byte. A bit has a value of 1 and the maximum value of a byte is 255 in base 10. We use 8-digit codes rather than 6- or 10-digit ones because the Z80 in microprocessor is designed as an "8-bit" processor, which means it can handle eight bits worth of data (numerical information)—no more and no less. So, as far as data is concerned we are restricted to a maximum of 255. You can test this by typing POKE 100, 365. The computer will reject it and give an error message.

Let us look now at the way in which we command the computer when POKEing. We start with the address of the particular byte in memory, and follow this with the number to be POKEd into it. We can think of the computer's memory as a lot of little boxes, all of which have their own binary number (the address of the box), and something in it (the contents).

As we said a little earlier, with only one byte, eight bits, the maximum number we can have on the Timex Sinclair is 11111111 or 255 (base 10). We can live with that when it comes to the contents, but imagine what it would be like if everybody's house address was between 0 and 255. What we do for computer locations is very similar to adding street names to house addresses, but they are actually numbers. For example, after going through the first 256(0–255) addresses, we say that the "street name" is 1 and go through the numbers 0–255 once again. So the final address looks like this:

00010110   01011010
"street name"   "house number"

We can now see that because there are 256 street names and 256 house numbers we have $256 \times 256 = 65536$ addresses. Technically this is known as a "16-bit" number, and has many advantages, mainly because we can actually think of it as one long number with 16 bits. For example: if we have a number such as 10101101 and we wish to add it to 10010001 we find that it overflows.

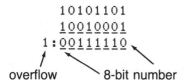

But if we use 16-bit registers then the overflow is no problem:

00000000   10101101
00000000   10010001
00000001   00111110

This means that we can quite happily multiply two numbers with the knowledge that the result would have to be over 65535 before the overflow comes into operation.

Going back to addresses, we can see that this is why, with the Z80 which uses 16-bit address codes, the maximum number of addresses it can cope with is 65535.

RAM stands for Random Access Memory, and ROM stands for Read Only Memory. If we consider a "location" in memory as a house, we can say that with RAM you can look through the windows and see the contents and open the door and change it. But with ROM you can look through the windows and "read" it, but the door is locked so you cannot go in and change it.

Handling binary numbers is far too complicated for ordinary use. This is where our third and most important base comes in, base 16. With this base, an 8-digit binary number can be written down to a 2-digit base 16, or hexadecimal number. You'll recall that a number in base 2 has digits of 0 and 1, and with base 10 a number is written with digits between 0 and 9, so base 16 should have digits between 0 and 15. However, we haven't got any digits bigger than 9. We use the first six letters of the alphabet:

        10 = A
        11 = B
        12 = C
        13 = D
        14 = E
        15 = F

The simplest way of converting an 8-bit binary number into hexadecimal or base 16 is to separate the eight bits into two groups of four bits and convert each group into a single character and then combine the two characters. For example:

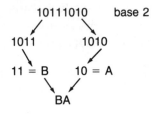

Hence we can now convert any value of a byte into a 2-digit hexadecimal number. This is the most convenient and most common way of representing a single byte.

The table below shows the equivalent binary, decimal and hexadecimal numbers.

Decimal	Hexadecimal	Binary
0	0	0000
1	1	0001
2	2	0010
3	3	0011
4	4	0100
5	5	0101
6	6	0110
7	7	0111
8	8	1000
9	9	1001
10	A	1010
11	B	1011
12	C	1100
13	D	1101
14	E	1110
15	F	1111

Now that we basically understand the mathematics of machine code (the boring part), we can move into actual programming.

The Z80 itself only understands numerical codes rather than actual instructions. What we do is write our program or routine using a *mnemonic* or instruction word, and then covert this to a number or group of numbers which can be POKEd into the computer in their decimal form and executed by a USR routine. For example, enter this into your Timex Sinclair:

```
CLEAR 32000
```

This clears a space from location 32000 to the top of RAM (32767 on the 16K and 65535 on the 48K). This also protects your routine from the computer writing over it with a BASIC program or NEWing it. This is the first address at which our machine code routine can be safely situated, 32000. The next problem is to get our machine code into this area of RAM. The way we do this is simply by POKEing the values in.

Try this:

```
POKE 32000, 1  (then press ENTER)
POKE 32001, 0
POKE 32002, 0
POKE 32003, 201
```

Now type PRINT USR 32000 and it will print 0. POKEing numbers in like this is ideal for just a few numbers, but if you have 30 or more it gets tedious. There are two ways of simplifying the task:

1. a FOR/NEXT loop:

   ```
   10 FORa=32000TO32003: INPUTx:POKEa,x:
   NEXTa
   ```

2. Using DATA statements:

   ```
   5 RESTORE
   10 FORa=32000 to 32003: READx: POKEa,x:
   NEXTa
   20 DATA 1,0,0,201
   ```

Both these methods have their particular applications, but I prefer the second method using a DATA statement because you can easily look at, and, if necessary modify it.

Here is a program for loading machine code into the Timex Sinclair:

```
10   INPUT "Start address?";start
20   CLEAR start
25   RESTORE
30   LET start=1 + (PEEK 23730 + 256*PEEK 23731)
40   FOR a=start TO 65535
     (use 32767 on a 16K Timex Sinclair)
```

```
50   READ x: IF x=999 THEN STOP
60   POKE a,x
70   NEXT a
80   DATA . . . you put your routine here . . .
```

Let's look at the program line by line to see how it works: Line 10 asks for the start location of the program. We discussed the start location earlier. 20 CLEARs space at, and above, this location. 25 RESTOREs the DATA pointer to the first element of DATA. 30 reassigns the variable "start" to its original value. This is necessary because CLEAR wipes all variables. 40 starts a loop between our start location and the maximum possible address on the Timex Sinclair (65535 on a 48K machine, 32767 on a 16K one). 50 READs the first element of DATA and checks whether it is 999, which is an illegal code for POKEing, so we use it to identify the end of the DATA. 60 loads or POKEs the address with the contents (x) which have just been read from the DATA statement. 70 repeats the loop. 80 holds the decimal values of all the instructions in your routine, and ends with a 999. It is not necessary to have all the DATA in one line. You can use as many as you like, subject to available memory.

So this routine loads the machine code into RAM. To run it we either include the line PRINT USR start or RANDOMIZE USR start within our program. USR is a BASIC command (which you get from the L key), and stands for User SubRoutine.

There are no variables, as such, in machine code. Instead there are "registers" which can be loaded, read and manipulated. Here is a simple sketch of the Z80 registers:

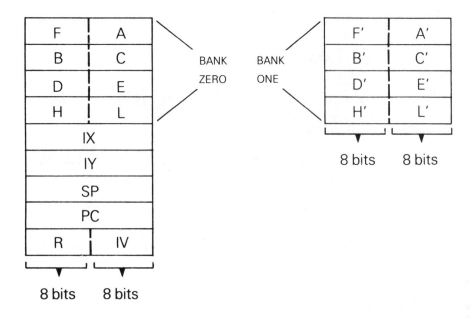

Each of the single letter registers (B,C,B',C,'D and the like) are 8-bit or single byte registers, but are designed to be combined to make 16-bit registers. The registers in bank zero, except for F, can be used by you in any way you like. F is used by the computer for its own operations, and therefore should not be altered.

Register pairs 1X and 1Y are index registers which we'll leave alone for the time being. SP is the Stack Pointer which is used by the computer, but can be used to advantage by an experienced machine code programmer.

PC is the Program Counter which holds the location in memory where the last executed instruction is situated. Register R is another one used by the computer, and has an apparently random value. It is possible to change this value, but because it is used for a specific purpose this is rarely done.

The registers in bank one can be used by you, but are not particularly easy to manipulate. For the time being, we will concentrate on the use of the registers in bank zero, except for F (that is, A,B,C,D,E,H and L).

As I said earlier, all these registers are simple 8-bit/one-byte registers, with a maximum value of 255. However, Z80 machine code was written so it is simple to create register pairs by combining B and C, D and E, and H and L (BC, DE and HL) which can then be treated as 16-bit registers. As you may recall from our earlier discussion, this gives us the range zero to 65535.

From discussing the existence of register pairs, we'll move to an explanation of how to put what we want into them. To load a single register with a number we use an instruction of the form: LD register, number. So, if we wanted to load register A (the Accumulator, as it is called) with the value 1, the machine code instruction would be:

```
LD A,01
```

We can do the same thing on any of the single registers: A, B, C, D, E, H or L:

```
LD B,255
```

The number loaded into a register must lie between zero and 255. If we then decide to treat D and E as a register pair (DE), we can handle it in the same way:

```
LD DE,1025
```

In this case we can use any number in the range zero to 65535.

We must remember that we have to convert a statement of the form LD B,255 into a decimal code before we can put it into the computer. Here is a table of LD commands, and their codes, with xxx being a number between zero and 255:

```
LD  A,xxx                62xxx
LD  B,xxx                06xxx
LD  D,xxx                22xxx
LD  E,xxx                30xxx
LD  C,xxx                14xxx
LD  H,xxx                38xxx
LD  L,xxx                46xxx
LD  BC,xxx  xxx          01xxx  xxx
LD  DE,xxx  xxx          17xxx  xxx
LD  HL,xxx  xxx          33xxx  xxx
```

Not only can you load a register with a number, but you can also load one register with the value of another. For example LD A,B means load the register A with the value of register B. Unfortunately, there are no commands to load one register pair with the contents of another. Therefore, if you want to load HL with BC, it is necessary to do the following:

```
LD  H,B
LD  L,C
```

Note that there are no line numbers, as such, in machine code. So, if you want to JumP or perform a loop, you have to JumP to an address. But before we do any JumPing, there are a couple of other things you can quite easily do to registers.

For example, if you want to subtract a number from register A, you do this:

```
SUB  A,01
```

which means LET A=A – 1 or SUBtract 1 from A. You can also subtract other registers from register A:

```
SUB  A,B
```

The codes for all the instructions are listed in most machine code books written for the Z80 processor.

After you've called a machine code routine, that is, after you've told the computer to PRINT USR . . . or RANDOMIZE USR . . . , you need an instruction in machine code to tell the computer to return to using BASIC. It is much the same as when you use the GOSUB command in BASIC; you need a RETURN to get back to the main program. The command you use to get back to BASIC from machine code is RET, which has a decimal code of 201.

There's one more thing I'd like to point out before you'll be ready to embark on the rewarding task of actually writing your own machine code routines. If you type PRINT USR xxx, the number printed will be the value of the register pair BC after the routine. So if we carried out the following routine:

```
LD  B,0
LD  C,0
RET
```

which we could do by using the machine code loader given earlier, and the values 06,0,14,00,201,999; and then entered PRINT USR 32000, we'd get the value of the register pair BC, which—not surprisingly—will be zero (as the routine has loaded BC with zero).

Now try playing around with the values of the second and fourth bytes. These are the ones which control B and C. The value of B is the number of 256's, and C is the remainder (between 0 and 255). When you work out the code for a register pair loading (LD HL, xxx xxx) it is important to remember that it takes the value for the remainder (L or Low Byte) first and then the number of 256's (H or High Byte). For example, if the number of 256's is zero, and there is a remainder of 100, H equals zero, and L equals 100. Using mnemonics we'd write LD HL,000 100 which in decimal would be 33 100 000. Note that the numbers are swapped around when it comes to coding them in decimal form.
Try this:

```
LD  B,0     0600
LD  C,0     1400
LD  A,12    6212
SUB  A,6    21406
LD  C,A     79
RET         201
```

What this is doing is:

LD B,O Load B with 0

LD C,O Load C with 0

LD A,12 Load A with 12

SUB A,6 Subtract 6 from A

LD C,A Load C with the value in A

RET Return to BASIC

The BASIC equivalent would be:

```
LET  B  =  0
LET  C  =  0
LET  A  =  12
LET  A  =  A  -  6
LET  C  =  A
RETURN
```

The BASIC version takes over 60 bytes of memory. The machine code one takes just 10 bytes, and is much faster.

This brings us to the end of this introduction to machine code. It was not intended to turn you into a master machine code programmer, but rather to give you a basic understanding of the principles involved and to give you a basis to build on.

Suggestions for Further Reading

Wadsworth, Nat. *Z80 Instruction Handbook.* Scelbi Publications, 1978. This booklet explains, in easily understood terms, the capabilities of the Z80's instruction set. It serves as a reference to the standard mnemonics, machine code and usage for each type of instruction provided in the Z80 CPU. Mr. Wadsworth says: "It is meant to serve as a practical guide for the novice, intermediate, or professional programmer who has a requirement to work at the machine or assembler language level with a Z80 based microprocessor."

Wadsworth, Nat. *Z80 Software Gourmet Guide and Cookbook.* Scelbi Publications, 1979. This book contains a complete description of the Z80's instruction set, and a wide variety of programming information in the form of useable routines.

9
■

A Guide to Better Programming

In computer programming, as in most areas of human accomplishment, a value system has been developed which classes certain techniques as "good," "not so good" or "bad." In the early days of working with your Timex Sinclair, the fact that you could get a working program which did, more or less, what you intended is a significant achievement in itself. But as you spend more time programming, you may perhaps think it worthwhile to try and improve your technique. Doing this will not only make programs easier to debug, but it will be much simpler to work out which particular section of code is supposed to achieve what end. If you want to further develop a program later on, a properly structured one will be much easier to work on than one which is a convoluted mass of leap-frogging GO TOs, and long strings of IF THENs. A well-written program is also easier to use.

However, the rules are not engraved on tablets of stone. I do not accept all of them unquestioningly, and I do not suggest that you do either. The use of unconditional GO TO commands, for example, is considered the height of poor taste in programming, but in a BASIC such as that provided on the Timex Sinclair which does not have procedures, REPEAT/UNTIL or DO/WHILE, GO TO can often not be avoided. However, it is worth looking at any unconditional GO TOs in your programs to see if they can be avoided, either by moving whole blocks of code to another position within the program, or by use of a subroutine, or a FOR/NEXT loop.

There is another example of the law of good programming practice which can often be safely ignored on the Timex Sinclair. It is considered pretty bad form to jump out of FOR/NEXT loops without letting them run their course. On some computers it is impossible to jump out of too many loops in a program without the whole thing crashing, but you can do so with impunity as many times as you like on the Timex Sinclair. And an uncompleted FOR/NEXT loop is a lesser sin than a lot of IF X = 3 THEN LET X = X + 1: GO TO Y statements which are often the only alternative to allowing FOR/NEXT loops to be exited prematurely.

Keep in mind then, when reading the rest of this chapter that the "rules" are more of the nature of suggestions or observations. Read them and think about them, but then feel completely free to ignore them if you think they are not the best idea to apply in a particular programming situation. However, the rules would not have evolved unless there were good reasons, so you may benefit from trying to apply them before you decide to discard them.

Many books on programming suggest you start with a flowchart which links boxes and diamonds containing decisions the computer must make with lines showing the flow of the program when it is running. Although it is not important to produce elaborate flow diagrams, you may well find that a rough flowchart is helpful in sorting out in your own mind, before you actually start punching code into your Timex Sinclair, exactly what it is you want the program to achieve.

Sometimes a series of key statements, perhaps linked by lines and arrows, is all you'll need. Such a series of statements for a BREAKOUT type of program, for example, might read: "Set up variables; print the initial bricks at the top of the screen; move the ball; read the keyboard to see if the player wants to move the bat; check if the ball has hit a wall and if it has deflect it; check if the ball has hit a brick and if it has erase the brick and increment the score; check if the ball is at the bottom of the screen and compare its position with the position of the bat; if the two coincide, let the ball bounce upward at a randomly-determined angle, if not, decrement the ball count by one, and see if the available balls have been used up; if so, go to the end of the game, if not, go back to the line which moves the ball, and continue cycling." If you wanted to, you could write a BREAKOUT program based just on this outline. If you started to write the program without any outline at all, you might get to the end and realize when you first ran it that you had left something quite important out. You would then either have to try and squeeze it in between other statements, add an ugly GO TO to put it at the very end, or try and get around it some other way.

Every time the Timex Sinclair comes to a GO TO or a GO SUB, it has to search the whole program from the very first line, line by line, until it finds the one designated. Therefore, the later in a program the line appears, the slower the program will run. The speed is only affected very slightly, but in a moving graphics program every delay can make the program less effective. Therefore, you should put often-called subroutines as close to the beginning of the program as you can. When the speed of the program is important, you could start the program with a REM statement giving the program its title, with the second line a GO SUB to, say, line 9000 where the variables would be initialized, and any instructions to the user could be given. This has two advantages. Firstly, it means that the computer does not have to go through all of the initialization and instruction routine every time it searches for a GO TO or GO SUB. Secondly, if you find, while writing a program, that you have left out a variable which is needed, you can easily add it to the end of the program before the final RETURN, rather than having to try and squeeze it in near the beginning.

Another aim to keep in mind when writing a program is that anyone using it should know, without doubt, what they are supposd to do. The program should either contain clear instructions, or they should be provided in some form with it. A combination of written instructions on a sheet of paper with a condensed version of them (such as telling the user which key to press to get which response) within the program is probably better than a vast sheaf of instructions actually within the program. This is not so important for a program intended solely for your own use, but is vital for programs which will be sold, or otherwise supplied for other people to run.

It is also important to add "mug traps" into your programs, to trap erroneous input before it causes a program crash. Ways of doing this are discussed in Chapter 5, on education, and mentioned in other places in the book. Techniques which allow the user a chance to examine input as entered before it is finally accepted by the program (such as in several programs in Chapter 4, on business,) are important in programs where a great deal of information must be entered. A final check and the chance to correct information which has been accepted, is also a good idea. Again, many of the programs in Chapter 4 include this facility.

Additionally, the program prompts should be fairly clear. A flashing cursor at the bottom of the screen shows that an input is expected, but unless something is either printed on the screen or included within the input statement, the user may be at a loss as to what must be entered. A separate written list of requirements in no way compensates for proper user prompts within the program. Many programs written on the Timex Sinclair's predecessors, the Timex Sinclair 1000 and 1500, could not afford the luxury of explicit user prompts due to a shortage of memory, but this excuse is generally not applicable to the Timex Sinclair.

REM statements, explaining what the following section is supposed to do, can help keep a listing transparent and ensure that when you return to it after a break you know what each section of the program is supposed to be doing. In Chapter 5, the CATS AND THINGS program shows the correct use of REM statements. Looking at the REM statements alone tells you just about all you need to know about the program. If you needed to, you could probably construct the whole program yourself just from the

REM statements: CHOOSE AND FORM OBJECT; PRINT RND NO OF OBJECTS; CORRECTION SEQUENCE; PRAISE; SINGLE KEY INPUT; DATA. There is no doubt that a program which incudes REM statements is easier to unravel than one which does not.

Once you've worked out what your program is meant to do and have written a list of the main parts of the program, make a list of the parts of each part. By breaking down each routine into smaller routines, you'll find the program practically writes itself. You will also be alerted to possible errors and omissions, even before you've entered a single line of code. It may be worth keeping a separate sheet of paper on hand while you're doing this, to note the variables which will be needed. Then, when you come to set up the "assign variables" section of your program, you'll already have a list of the ones you need.

You'll find it easier to work out what is happening in a program if you use explicit variable names, like SCORE for score, and HISCORE for high score, and so on. Although these take a little longer to type than do single letter variables, they minimize the chance of using the same letter twice within a long program for different things, which can cause hard-to-trace program breakdowns. Longer variable names also, of course, use up more memory than do single letter names, but this is unlikely to be a problem with most programs you write on the Timex Sinclair. You'll see in several of the business programs, such as FINANCIAL MODEL, how useful explicit variable names can be. In this program, for example, variable names include TOTAL, AVERAGE and NUMBER.

In general, do not re-invent the wheel. Although you should not steal or adapt programs and then try to pass them off as your own, there is little point in spending hours of programming time working out, for example, a numerical sort routine, when a number of suitable routines are already available in publications. It is quite likely, anyway, that you'll end up producing an identical routine to one which you could have lifted or adapted in the first place, as there is a limited number of ways to carry out certain tasks. This suggestion only applies if you are in a particular hurry to get a program finished. The satisfaction you will gain by writing a routine from scratch, no matter how standard it is, and the greater insight you are likely to have into its operation, will more than repay the time invested in most cases. So, if you have time, re-inventing the wheel may be worthwhile.

Many programmers become proficient fairly quickly in using certain parts of Timex Sinclair BASIC, but once they have mastered this, they put the manual away and do not continue exploring the other statements and commands available in the language. No matter how familiar you become with your Timex Sinclair and its version of BASIC you should look through the manual (and this and other books on the computer) from time to time, just to see if there is some aspect of it which you have either misunderstood or of which you know nothing.

You may find it easier and more instructive to mentally "run" parts of a program as though you were the computer, than it would be to just press RUN. Start at the beginning of the program and follow the instructions as you come to them. When you are acting as the computer in this way, you'll often discover clumsily written routines or ones which are potential trouble spots, that might not show up when the Timex Sinclair is running the program. "Hand-running" a program is also a good time to determine if, at any point, the computer will try to do something like divide by zero that would cause the program to halt with an error message.

Make sure the program output is clear to the user. You cannot write a program assuming that you'll be looking over the user's shoulder every time the program is run. A program which needs you to say things like "That figure in the top right hand corner is the number of attempts you've made so far to guess the answer" or "The first number you see is the result of the year's sales and the second is projected sales for the second month" could hardly be described as well-written.

The suggestions put forward in this chapter fall into two main areas:

- Thinking before starting to program.
- Working out how the program interacts (both in accepting input and in outputting results) with a user who did not write the program.

If you carry out your programming with the intention of doing the best you can in both these areas, you're likely to find the quality of your programming work improves almost immediately, and will continue to improve.

Suggestions for Further Reading

Ledin, George and Ledin, Victor. *The Programmer's Book of Rules.* Belmont, Ca.: Wadsworth, Lifetime Learning Publications, 1979.

Meek, Brian and Heath, Patricia, eds. *Guide to Good Programming Practice.* Chichester: Ellis Horwood Ltd./John Wiley & Sons, 1980.

Nagin, Paul A. and Ledgard, Henry F. *BASIC With Style.* Rochelle Park, N.J.: Hayden Book Company, 1978.

Savage, Earl R. *BASIC Programmer's Notebook.* Indianapolis: Howard Sams & Co., 1982.

Appendix A

History

Your Timex Sinclair is one of the latest stages in the long road which humanity has traveled in the attempt at building calculating machines. The earliest "machine" was probably the abacus, which used parallel rods on a frame. The position of beads on the rods indicated a particular number. The abacus was used up until very recently, when it was superseded by the pocket calculator.

John Napier, from Scotland, is one of the earliest figures we can identify who contributed to the production of "calculating machines." Napier invented what became known as "Napier's Bones," nine four-sided segmented rods which allowed multiplication to be performed by adding together numbers displayed on the rods. The English clergyman William Oughtred developed a primitive slide rule in 1621, which multiplied numbers—as do all subsequent slide rules—by adding lengths related to the logarithms of those numbers.

Later in the seventeenth century, Blaise Pascal developed a method of adding numbers together using interlocking wheels. He put the wheels in a box, with little windows to display the result of a calculation after you "dialed" the numbers you wished to add. Gottfried Leibniz, a contemporary of Pascal, worked out a way to mechanize multiplication. His method was so good it was still being used in calculating machines 250 years later.

In 1792, Charles Babbage was born in Devon. He is a major figure in the history of computers. In fact, many say he invented the very first one. Babbage was unhappy with the mathematical tables available in his day, and tried to build a "difference engine" which would work out more accurate ones. He was let down by the inability of the engineers of his day to build parts to the accuracy required. Babbage lost interest in his difference engine, and began the construction of an "analytical engine" which, if it had worked as planned, would have been the first computer: a calculating machine which could carry out any kind of calculation and which would be able to make decisions on what it would do next as a result of results obtained during the calculation.

The mathematics which lies behind computers' ability to make decisions is called Boolean algebra. It was devised—long before present-day computers were conceived—by the English mathematician and logician George Boole. In 1890, punched cards were used for the first time to record and tabulate an American census. The card system was developed by Herman Hollerith, who formed a company to sell his system. The company prospered, swallowed up competitors, and eventually was renamed the International Business Machine Corporation, now the biggest computer company in the world, IBM.

In the 1870s, a British physicist Lord Kelvin developed a device to predict tide times, and later suggested that a machine which he called the "differential analyser" could be built which would solve not only tide prediction problems, but general problems associated with the solution of differential equations. Such a machine was built in 1930 by a professor at the Massachusetts Institute of Technology, Vannevar Bush. Although the machine worked, Bush realized that there was no future in mechanical calculating machines, and replaced parts of his machine with valves. The modern computer moved another step closer to reality.

In the 1940's, George Stibitz, who was working for Bell Telephone Laboratories, discovered that binary information (information stored as a pattern of ones and zeroes) could be represented and manipulated by a series of switches, with *on* representing one, and *off* representing zero. A device he rigged up using telephone relays and little lights was the world's first electronic calculator, and pointed the way to the use of binary arithmetic in computers. Nearly all modern computers use binary arithmetic, which the computer generally translates into numbers and letters we can understand.

Although the idea of the first computer was outlined in Cambridge, England in 1832, it was not until 1944, in Cambridge, Massachusetts, that the idea actually came into being. The first fully automatic calculating machine, the Automatic Sequence Controlled Calculator, was completed in that year by Howard Aiken of Harvard, working for IBM.

Early computers took up a great deal of space, used vast amounts of electricity to power all their valves and were notoriously unreliable. The transistor, invented in 1947, did much to reduce the size of computers, but it was not until the first *microprocessor* (the thing we now know as a *chip*) was built in 1971, that tiny computers of today, such as the Sinclair, became possible.

The idea of the integrated circuit, the forerunner of the chip, was first suggested by G. W. Dummer, who worked for the British Royal Radar Establishment. Nobody took much notice of the idea, and it wasn't until six years later that an American, Jack Kilby, working for Texas Instruments, actually made the first one.

The American company Intel made the historic first microprocessor, known as the 4004, in November 1971. Intel, and the world, did not realize at first the enormous social impact their product would have. It took almost a year before people began to realize that the seeds for a revolution which could transform the world had been sown.

The first personal computer, the Altair, was built by a small New Mexico company, Mits, in 1975. The race to produce ever smaller, ever more powerful personal computers was underway. Clive Sinclair entered that race in the late seventies.

Clive Sinclair had founded his first company, Sinclair Radionics, in 1962 to produce radio and amplifier kits for sale through mail order advertisements. By 1967, the company was turning over around £100,000 a year, and the range of products had expanded to include hi-fi systems. Five years later Sinclair entered the calculator market with the Executive, the world's first pocket calculator, which made world headlines. The world's media took note again in January, 1977 with the launch of Sinclair's Microvision, the world's first "pocket" television, with a tiny, two-inch screen. Two years later, a British version selling at less than half the cost of the first model was produced.

At the end of January, 1980, Clive Sinclair released his first computer, the ZX80. It was the cheapest computer in the world at the time, and seems to have played a major part in bringing down the prices of small computers generally since that time. With the launch of the somewhat limited ZX80 in 1980, Sinclair became almost overnight Britain's largest microcomputer manufacturer. With the release of its successor, the much more flexible ZX81, just over a year later, Sinclair gained the world title.

The Spectrum, the Timex Sinclair in the U.S., which had its British launch in April, 1982, is a worthy successor to the ZX81, offering similar computing power to the ZX81 (although it runs far more quickly), but with added features such as color, sound, and high resolution graphics. Its release triggered a wave of price reductions in other small color computers and a number of rivals to the Spectrum were soon announced.

Suggestions for Further Reading

Bradbeer, Robin. *The Personal Computer Book.* Gower Publishing Co., 1982.

Buchsbaum, Walter H. *Personal Computers Handbook.* Indianapolis: Howard W. Sams & Co., 1981.

Bunnell, David. *Personal Computing, a Beginner's Guide.* New York: Dutton, 1978.

Ditlea, Steve. *A Simple Guide to Home Computers.* Skokie, Ill.: A & W Visual Library, 1979.

Evans, Christopher. *The Making of the Micro.* Gollancz, 1982.

Hartnell, Tim. *The Personal Computer Guide.* Virgin Books, 1982.

Lavington, Simon. *Early British Computers.* Manchester: Manchester University Press, 1980.

Solomon, Leslie and Veit, Stanley. *Getting Involved With Your Own Computer.* Hillside, N.J.: Enslow Publishers, 1977.

Appendix B

Peripherals

Peripherals is the jargon word for "things which are attached to the computer without actually being part of it." The most important peripherals are human input devices (e.g., keyboard, built into most computers nowadays), human-readable output devices (screen, printer), and mass storage devices (such as a disc or tape). Most large computers have slave computers which handle their interface with the real world (peripheral processors). The slaves are generally a lot bigger than the Timex Sinclair.

An RS232 network interface board is available for the Timex Sinclair which allows you to connect the computer to a very wide range of printers, terminals and other computers. The RS232 is one of the standard interfaces available, which is why so many RS232-compatible devices have been made.

PRINTERS

A printer is needed for most serious applications. Types of printer and relevant bits of jargon include:

Line printer: a large, expensive device which prints a whole line at a time, typically at a rate in excess of 600 lines of 132 characters per minute. Used with larger computers.

Daisywheel and golfball: complete characters are formed by impact, as by a typewriter.

Dot matrix: characters are made up of an array of dots, produced by impact, thermally, or electrostatically.

Impact: the print mechanism physically strikes an inked ribbon which marks the paper.

Thermal: special paper which blackens when heated; the printer very rapidly heats and cools a pinpoint area of paper at a time.

Electrostatic: aluminum-coated silvery paper; the printer generates sparks which expose a black backing.

You pay for speed and good print quality. Thermal and electrostatic paper is expensive, although the printers themselves are cheaper. If you simply want to get information out as cheaply as possible (and not in large quantities), the Timex Sinclair printer for the Timex Sinclair is perfectly satisfactory.

MEMORY, OR MASS STORAGE DEVICES (MSDs)

The most common mass storage devices are magnetic tape and magnetic disc. For cassette recording of Timex Sinclair programs, you'll probably find mono portables are best. Try to avoid using a machine with a stereo head. If you can, try to get a machine known to give good results with computers (not necessarily an expensive one). Use power from a standard AC outlet rather than battery power (if you get bad results with AC outlet power, use a different recorder). Useful frills for tape use include a tape counter; manual (rather than the ubiquitous automatic) level control; recording level meter; cue and review facilities; a suitable tape loading aid to set levels and check for dropouts. A tone contol is definitely undesirable; if your recorder has one, keep it set to its maximum position. In many cases it is best not to plug in the earphone and microphone leads simultaneously.

Use good tape, never longer than C60. TDK type D is excellent. BASF, Agfa, etc., all produce satisfactory tapes. Good C12 and C15 tapes as sold for computer use are the best, but not all of these tapes are of high enough quality. A tape loading aid will help you to check on the quality of a tape by recording a program and monitoring the level fluctuations.

Discs are much faster than tapes. They also allow information anywhere on the disc to be found fast (no rewinding). You can read from several files in rapid sequence and it is possible to alternate operations on different files on the same disc (e.g. read details on a stock line, update the information, write the new information to another file or even to the same one. On tape this would be impossible: it would require constant precise rewinding).

The Microdrive, a miniature floppy disc, can hold up to 100K of information. Up to eight at a time can be connected to the Timex Sinclair. Information is transferred to and from the Microdrive at an incredible 16K a second, whereas the transfer rate to a cassette tape is around 1.5K a second.

Mass storage is never completely reliable; it is *vital* to keep backup copies of valuable information. To a certain extent original information and printed output can be used as a last ditch safeguard; you will not rely heavily on this after you have had to re-enter three months' worth of orders manually. Backups need not be on the same MSD as the working copy; discs can be backed up on tape, for example. Keep backups at a different location from the working copies. Remember that the information stored can often be much more valuable than the computer system itself. If traveling by train or subway, don't put magnetic media on the floor near motors. Never assume without checking that the disc or tape you are going to erase and rewrite is actually the right one.

Appendix C

Timex Sinclair Specifications

DIMENSIONS

Width 37.5 cm
Depth 19 cm
CPU/Memory

Z80A microprocessor running at 3.5 MHz. 16K-byte ROM containing BASIC interpreter and operating system. 16K-byte RAM (plus optional 32K-byte RAM on internal expansion board) or 48K-byte RAM.

KEYBOARD

41-key keyboard with upper and lower case with capitals lock feature. All BASIC words obtained by single keys, plus 16 graphics characters, 22 color control codes and 21 user-definable graphics characters. All keys have auto repeat.

DISPLAY

Memory-mapped display of 256 pixels × 176 pixels; plus one attributes byte per character square, defining one of eight foreground colors, one of eight background colors, normal or extra brightness and flashing or steady. Screen border color also settable to one of eight colors.

SOUND

Internal loudspeaker can be operated over more than 10 octaves (actually 130 semitones) via BASIC BEEP command. Jack sockets at the rear of computer allow connections to external amplifier/speaker.

GRAPHICS

Point, line, circle and arc drawing commands in high-resolution graphics. Sixteen pre-defined graphics characters plus 21 user-definable graphics characters. Also functions to yield character at a given position, attribute at a given position (colors, brightness and flash) and whether a given pixel is set. Text may be written on the screen on 24 lines of 32 characters. Text and graphics may be freely mixed.

COLORS

Foreground and background colors, brightness and flashing are set by BASIC INK, PAPER, BRIGHT and FLASH commands. OVER may also be set, which performs an exclusive-or operation to overwrite any printing or plotting that is already on the screen. INVERSE will give inverse video printing. These six commands may be set globally to cover all further PRINT, PLOT, DRAW or CIRCLE commands, or locally within these commands to cover only the results of that command. They may also be set locally to cover text printed by an INPUT statement. Color-control codes, which may be accessed from the keyboard, may be inserted into text or program listing, and when displayed will override the globally set colors until another control code is encountered. Brightness and flashing codes may similarly be inserted into program or text. Color-control codes in a program listing have no effect on its execution. Border color is set by a BORDER command. The eight colors available are black, blue, red, magenta, green, cyan, yellow and white. All eight colors may be present on the screen at once, with some areas flashing and others steady, and any area may be highlighted.

SCREEN

The screen is divided into two sections. The top section—normally the first 22 lines—displays the program listing or the results of program or command execution. The bottom section—normally the last two lines—

shows the command or program line currently being entered or the program line currently being edited. It also shows the report messages. Full editing facilities of cursor left cursor right, insert and delete (with auto-repeat facility) are available over this line. The bottom section will expand to accept a current line of up to 22 lines.

MATHEMATICAL OPERATIONS AND FUNCTIONS

Arithmetic operations of $+$, $-$, $\times$, $\div$, and "raise to a power." Mathematical functions of sine, cosine, tangent and their inverses, natural logs and exponentials; sign function, absolute value function, and integer function; square root function, random number generation, and pi.

Numbers are stored as five bytes of floating point binary—giving a range of $\pm 3 \times 10^{-39}$ to $\pm 7 \times 10^{38}$ accurate to $9\frac{1}{2}$ decimal digits. Binary numbers may be entered directly with the BIN function. The symbols $=$, $>$, $<$, $>=$, $<=$ and $<>$ may be used to compare string or arithmetic values or variables to yield 0 (false) or 1 (true). Logical operators AND, OR and NOT yield Boolean results but will accept 0 (false) and any number (true).

User-definable functions are defined using DEF FN, and called using FN. They may take up to 26 numeric and 26 string arguments, and may yield string or numeric results.

There is a full DATA mechanism, using the commands READ, DATA and RESTORE.

A real-time clock is obtainable.

STRING OPERATIONS AND FUNCTIONS

Strings can be concatenated with $+$. String variables or values may be compared with $=$, $>$, $<$, $>=$, $<=$ and $<>$ to give Boolean results. String functions are VAL, VAL$, STR$ and LEN. CHR$ and CODE convert numbers to characters and vice versa, using the ASCII code. A string slicing mechanism exists, using the form a$(xTOv).

VARIABLE NAMES

Numeric—any string starting with a letter (upper and lower case are not distinguished between, and spaces are ignored).
String—A$ to Z$
FOR/NEXT loops—A–Z
Numeric arrays—A–Z
String arrays—A$ to Z$
Simple variables and arrays with the same name are allowed and distinguished between.

ARRAYS

Arrays may be multi-dimensional, with subscripts starting at 1. String arrays, technically character arrays, may have their last subscript omitted, yielding a string.

EXPRESSION EVALUATOR

A full expression evaluator is called during program execution whenever an expression, constant or variable is encountered.

This allows the use of expressions as arguments to GO TO, GO SUB, etc. It also operates on commands allowing the Timex Sinclair to operate as a calculator.

CASSETTE INTERFACE

A tone leader is recorded before the information to overcome the automatic recording level fluctuations of some tape recorders, and a Schmitt trigger is used to remove noise on playback. All saved information is started with a header containing information as to its type, title, length and address information. Program, screens, blocks of memory, string and character arrays may all be saved separately. Programs, blocks of memory and arrays may be verified after saving. Programs and arrays may be merged from tape to combine them with the existing contents of memory. Where two line numbers or variables names coincide, the old one is overwritten. Programs may be saved with a line number, where execution will start immediately on loading. The cassette interface runs at 1500 baud (bits per second), through two 3.5mm jack plugs.

EXPANSION PORT

This has the full data, address and control busses from the Z80A, and is used to interface to the ZX Printer, the RS232 and NET interfaces and the ZX Microdrives. IN and OUT commands give the I/O port equivalents of PEEK and POKE.

Index